GIVEN IN MEMORY
OF
ROBERT F. PECOR

GREAT BATTLES
THROUGH THE AGES

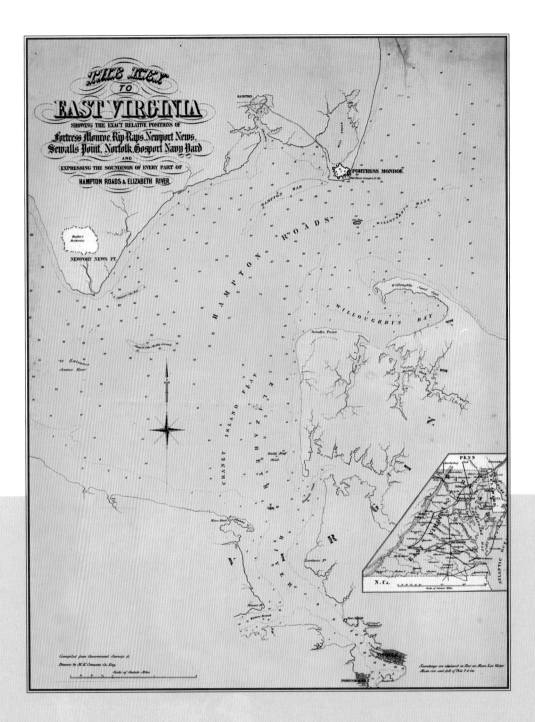

THE KEY
TO
EAST VIRGINIA
SHOWING THE EXACT RELATIVE POSITIONS OF
Fortress Monroe, Rip Raps, Newport News,
Sewalls Point, Norfolk, Gosport Navy Yard
AND
EXPRESSING THE SOUNDINGS OF EVERY PART OF
HAMPTON ROADS & ELIZABETH RIVER

HAMPTON

FORTRESS MONROE

HAMPTON BAR

WILLOUGHBYS BANK

H A M P T O N   R O A D S

Butler's Batteries

NEWPORT NEWS PT.

WILLOUGHBY'S BAY

Sewalls Point

Entrance
James River

C H A N E Y   I S L A N D   F L A T

Bush's Bluff

N. Ca.

V
I
R

V

River Branch

PENN

N. Ca.

ATLANTIC OCEAN

NORFOLK

PORTSMOUTH

Compiled from Government Surveys &
Drawn by M. K. Connest, Co. Eng.
Scale of Statute Miles

Soundings are expressed in Feet at Mean Low Water
Mean rise and fall of Tide 2 & in

GREAT
BATTLES
THROUGH
THE AGES

THE *MONITOR*
VS.
THE *MERRIMACK*

BRUCE L. BRAGER

INTRODUCTION BY
CASPAR W. WEINBERGER

CHELSEA HOUSE
PUBLISHERS
A Haights Cross Communications Company
Philadelphia

FRONTIS: Hampton Roads, Virginia, site of the March 9, 1862, battle between the U.S.S. *Monitor* and the C.S.S. *Virginia*.

CHELSEA HOUSE PUBLISHERS

VP, PRODUCT DEVELOPMENT Sally Cheney
DIRECTOR OF PRODUCTION Kim Shinners
CREATIVE MANAGER Takeshi Takahashi
MANUFACTURING MANAGER Diann Grasse

STAFF FOR THE *MONITOR* vs. THE *MERRIMACK*

EXECUTIVE EDITOR Lee Marcott
PRODUCTION ASSISTANT Megan Emery
PICTURE RESEARCHER Sarah Bloom
SERIES & COVER DESIGNER Keith Trego
LAYOUT 21st Century Publishing and Communications, Inc.

©2004 by Chelsea House Publishers,
a subsidiary of Haights Cross Communications.
All rights reserved. Printed in China.

A Haights Cross Communications Company

http://www.chelseahouse.com

First Printing

1 3 5 7 9 8 6 4 2

Library of Congress Cataloging-in-Publication Data applied for.

ISBN 0-7910-7439-0 HC 0-7910-7792-6 PB

TABLE OF **CONTENTS**

INTRODUCTION

by Caspar W. Weinberger

There are many ways to study and teach history, which has perhaps been best defined as the "recording and interpretation of past events." Concentration can be on a compilation of major events, or on those events that help prove a theory of the author's. Or the "great man" theory can be applied to write the history of a country or an era, based on a study of the principal leaders or accepted geniuses who are felt to have shaped events that became part of the tapestry of history.

This new Chelsea House series adopts and continues the plan of studying six of the major battles and turning points of wars that did indeed shape much of the history of the periods before, during, and after those wars. By studying the events leading up to major battles and their results, inescapably one learns a great deal about the history of that period.

The first battle, chosen appropriately enough, is the Battle of Actium. There, in 31 B.C., the naval forces of Antony and Cleopatra, and those of Octavian, did battle off the northwest coast of Greece for control of the Roman world. Octavian's victory ended the Roman civil war and gave him unchallenged supremacy, leading to his designation as Augustus, Rome's first emperor. It is highly appropriate that the Battle of Actium be studied first for this series, because the battle was for many decades used as the starting point for a new era.

Next, in chronological order, is a study of the long years of battles between the forces of Richard the Lionhearted and Saladin. This Third Crusade, during the twelfth century, and the various military struggles for Acre and Jerusalem, was the background against which much of the history of modern Britain and Europe and the Middle East was played out.

Coming down to modern times, the series includes a study of the battle that forever changed naval warfare. This battle, the first between two ironclad warships, the *Monitor* and the *Merrimack*, ended the era of naval wars fought by great fleets of sail- or oar-powered ships, with their highly intricate maneuvers. After the *Monitor* and *Merrimack*, all naval battles became floating artillery duels with wholly different tactics and skills required.

The sinking of the German ship *Bismarck* during World War II was not so much a battle as a clear demonstration of the fact that a huge preponderance of naval force on one side could hunt down and destroy one of the most powerful battleships then afloat.

The continued importance of infantry warfare was demonstrated in the Battle of the Bulge, the final attempt of the German army, near the end of World War II, to stave off what in hindsight is now seen as the inevitable victory of the Allies.

The last battle in this series covers the Korean War—one of the most difficult and costly we have fought, and yet a war whose full story is very nearly forgotten by historians and teachers. The story of the Korean War embodies far more than simply the history of a war we fought in the 1950s. It is a history that is dominated by General Douglas MacArthur—but it is also a history of many of the foundation stores of American foreign and domestic policy in the past half century.

These six battles, and the wars of which they were a part, are well worth studying because, although they obviously cannot recount all of history from Actium to Korea, they can and do show the reader the similarities of many of those issues that drive people and governments to war. They also recount the development and changes in technologies by which people have acquired the ability to destroy their fellow creatures ever more effectively and completely.

With the invention and deployment of each new instrument of destruction, from the catapults that were capable of blasting great holes in the walls defending castles and forts, to today's nuclear weapons, the prediction has always been made that the effects and capability of each of those engines of destruction were so awful that their very availability would end war entirely. Thus far, those predictions have always been wrong, although as the full potential of nuclear weapons of mass destruction is increasingly better understood, it may well be that the very nature of these ultimate weapons will, indeed, mean that they will ever be used. However, the sheer numbers of these ultimate weapons possessed by many countries, and the possibilities of some of those countries falling under the dictatorship of some of the world's most dangerous leaders, combine to make imaginable a war that could indeed end the world. That is why the United States has expended so much to try to prevent countries such as Iraq and North Korea from continuing to be led by men as inherently dangerous as Saddam Hussein and Kim Sung Il, who are determined to acquire the world's most dangerous weapons.

An increasing knowledge of some of the great battles of the past that have so influenced history is essential unless we want to fulfill the old adage that those who forget history are likely to be condemned to repeat it—with all of its mistakes.

This old adage reminds us also that history is a study not just of great military victories, but also the story of battles lost and the many mistakes that were made by even the greatest of commanders.

After every engagement that involves American troops in action, even on a very small scale, the Pentagon conducts a "Lessons Learned" exercise. What went wrong? What should have been done differently? Did we need more troops, more artillery, more planes? Most important, could more lives of our own troops have been saved?

These mistakes or command errors are not only carefully studied and written about, but they form the basis for war games or exercises in which actual battle situations are re-fought—sometimes on paper—but frequently with troops re-enacting various parts of the combat action. These "lessons learned" exercises become a valuable part of the training of troops and are an even more valuable part of the training of leaders and commanders.

As we can all guess from the short discussions of some of those great battles in this series, there were many opportunities for different commanders and different plans to be used. Indeed, history is perhaps our greatest teacher, and a study of great battles is a great way to learn, even though each battle is different and there will be different lessons to be learned from the post-battle studies.

So, this Chelsea House series serves as a splendid beginning to our study of military history—a history that we must master if we want to see the expansion and success of our basic policy of maintaining peace with freedom.

It is not enough to consider threats to our security and our freedom. We must also be constantly ready to defend our freedom by keeping our ability to prevent any of those threats against us from materializing into real dangers. The study of great battles and how they were won, despite mistakes that have been made, is a vital part of our ability to keep peace with freedom.

BY: Caspar W. Weinberger
Chairman, FORBES Inc.
March 2003

Caspar W. Weinberger was the fifteenth U.S. secretary of defense, serving under President Ronald Reagan from 1981 to 1987.

The Fall of
the Gosport
Navy Yard

Fort Sumter at the entrance to the harbor of Charleston, South Carolina, as it looked before the Civil War. When Union forces refused Confederate demands to evacuate the fort on April 12, 1861, the Confederates opened fire. Four bloody years of war followed.

The American Civil War began on the morning of April 12, 1861. Confederate artillery shells arched over the waters of Charleston Harbor, South Carolina, headed toward Fort Sumter, the Union fort sitting conspicuously in the middle of the harbor. The Southern commander, with the impressive name of Pierre Gustave Toutant Beauregard, had warned the Union commander, Robert Anderson, that he would open fire on the fort if the Union troops did not leave. When the Union troops stayed, Beauregard kept his word and ordered his men to open fire.

Confederate army Captain George S. James was instructed to fire a shot at 4:30 A.M., as a signal to all Confederate batteries to open fire on Fort Sumter. James turned to Roger Pryor, a volunteer aide

11

to Beauregard and a former congressman from Virginia, who had resigned his seat on March 3, and offered him the chance to fire the first shot of the American Civil War. Pryor, an ardent secessionist who had strongly supported the Southern states' leaving the union and setting up their own country, visibly winced at taking the next step and declined the honor. He later said, "I could not fire the first gun of the war."[1]

A Union rescue fleet sat outside Charleston Harbor, prevented by a complicated series of natural underwater shoals and sandbars, and the lack of local pilots to guide them in, from coming to the fort's assistance. After about a day and half of shelling, many of the wooden buildings inside the fort were on fire and the ammunition was running out. Anderson had no choice but to surrender. The next day, he and his men were allowed to salute their flag before sailing to New York City on the rescue fleet—which now was given local pilots. The Civil War had started out as a very polite war.

No one was confirmed killed in the Battle of Fort Sumter. The American Civil War was gentler at the start. However, two Union soldiers were killed when a cannon blew up while they were firing a salute to the American flag.

The Civil War would get meaner as it progressed. The war would also get a lot bloodier, eventually killing one in 50 Americans. But it was not only a land war that started early on April 12, 1861; naval power would play a highly significant role. Ships would support Union efforts at conquering Confederate territory in the "western" theater, basically the states between Virginia and the Mississippi River. Ships would play a role on the high seas, as the Confederates attempted to import war materials and to destroy Union commerce. Likewise, the Lincoln administration did its best to protect Union commerce and destroy Confederate commerce with naval power.

Therefore, in the most famous naval engagement of the war, two odd-looking, even bizarre-looking ships—a cheese box on a raft and a floating barn, as they were described at the time—would duel for control of a key water crossroads. When their duel was finished, they had changed the course of naval and military history by making wooden warships— that is, most warships afloat at the time—obsolete.

This book tells the story of that fight, variously called the Battle of Hampton Roads, the *Monitor* versus the *Merrimack*, and the *Monitor* versus the *Virginia*.

THE CONFEDERATES TAKE THE GOSPORT NAVY YARD

The "action" in the area where the fight took place, the Hampton-Norfolk (Virginia) area, began almost immediately after the firing on Fort Sumter. On April 15, 1861, right after Fort Sumter surrendered, President Abraham Lincoln proclaimed the existence of a rebellion. He called for 75,000 militia troops to enter national service to put down a rebellion "too powerful to be suppressed by the ordinary course of judicial proceedings."[2] This call, and the Southern firing on Sumter, mobilized Northern support for the war and recruited many more men than Lincoln had requested. The fence-sitting slave states of Tennessee, Arkansas, North Carolina, and Virginia were already leaning toward secession. Crowds of people in these states celebrated the firing on Fort Sumter and its surrender, both before Lincoln's proclamation. However, Lincoln's call provided them with the final push toward secession. (Four other states that permitted slavery, Missouri, Kentucky, Delaware, and Maryland, remained in the Union throughout the war.)

Most important for this story were the actions of Virginia. The Virginia Secession Convention, which had not acted earlier, voted to secede on April 17, 1861. On

May 23, 1861, by approximately a three-to-one margin, voters of the state approved secession. Virginia's departure from the Union, and its almost immediate entrance into membership in the Confederacy, created major problems for the Union government.

The primary problem was that Washington, D.C.—the North's capital, and in the view of the Lincoln administration, the national capital as well—laid just across the Potomac River from enemy territory. This problem was solved just after midnight on May 24, 1861. Lincoln sent three regiments of Union troops across the river to occupy the hills overlooking Washington and the town of Alexandria, and to guard the Virginia side of several bridges across the river. The problem of the Hampton-Norfolk area was not so easy to solve.

The importance of the Hampton-Norfolk area of Virginia became clear to both sides on April 19, 1861, when Abraham Lincoln declared the start of a naval blockade of the Confederate coast, from South Carolina on to the Mexican border. Eight days later, this was extended to include North Carolina and Virginia. The blockade was part of what came to be known as the "Anaconda Plan," after the giant snake that squeezes its victims to death. The blockade was planned to intercept every vessel attempting to enter or leave the Confederacy. When the blockade neared full effectiveness (it was never perfect) and with Union troops to capture key areas of the South, the Confederacy would be closed off to the outside world and squeezed until it either gave up or collapsed.

The term "Anaconda Plan" was not a compliment but rather an insult to its creator, General-in-Chief (Commander of the U.S. army) Winfield Scott, and his proposals. Most critics thought Scott was overestimating the effort necessary to subdue the South. It turned out that when he called for the Anaconda Plan, and later for

Lieutenant General Winfield Scott, general-in-chief (commanding general) of the U.S. army, from 1841 to November 1, 1861. Scott, who was older than Washington, D.C., itself, created the "Anaconda Plan," the broad framework for Union victory in the Civil War. The blockade of Southern ports was a key part of this plan.

300,000 troops, Scott was vastly underestimating the effort that would be required.

The body of water between Norfolk to the south and Hampton to the north is still known as Hampton Roads. The area is still a major center for the U.S. navy and for commercial maritime traffic. During the American Civil War, control of this water crossroads by the South would provide an entry point to the James River for

Southern ships attempting to run, or get through, the Northern blockade and bring in war and luxury material not available in the South. The South could also prevent the James River, which led directly to Richmond, from being used for a waterborne attack on Richmond by Northern naval and army forces.

For the North, this area would provide a place to anchor, supply, and repair ships enforcing the blockade. Union control of Hampton Roads would also protect the route up the Chesapeake Bay to Washington, by way of the Potomac River, and to Baltimore. This was a strong motivation for the Union government, very sensitive to Washington's security during the Civil War, to at least deny control of this area to the South.

Northern control would also safeguard the highly important naval yard called the Norfolk Navy Yard. More correctly, this was the Gosport Navy Yard, and was actually located in a suburb of Portsmouth, across the Elizabeth River from Norfolk. This facility was the largest and most important navy yard in the country. The yard contained a large granite dry dock that enabled major repairs to be undertaken on the parts of a ship's hull normally underwater. The Gosport Yard also contained three shipbuilding slips, a foundry, and other support services. More importantly, 1,200 naval cannons, at least 300 of the most modern types, were at Gosport. Twelve vessels were either stationed at the yard or undergoing repair, including the U.S.S. *Merrimack*.

Union forces controlled the northern shore of Hampton Roads. The most important Union installation was the huge Fort Monroe, built many years before on Old Point Comfort at the entrance to Hampton Roads from the Chesapeake Bay. The Union also securely held the village of Hampton and the area called Newport News. The Gosport Navy Yard, however, was located to the south of Hampton Roads. Norfolk and Portsmouth, and virtually the entire southern shore of the Roads, were very pro-Confederate. Lincoln and Union Secretary of the Navy Gideon Welles feared for the security of the ships and the cannons and equipment in the yard, and for the yard itself.

They were particularly concerned about the U.S.S. *Merrimack*, a relatively new and powerful warship. Both sails and engines powered this ship. Despite the fact that the engines often needed repair—which is why the ship was at Gosport—it was considered "state-of-the-art" among naval vessels.

Lincoln and Welles hesitated to send Union troops to the area, however, for fear of provoking Virginia to declare itself out of the Union—at least until the Virginia Secession Convention voted to secede. Lincoln and Welles were still feeling their way through a tense and difficult period, when any wrong move could have produced drastically bad consequences. The president and the secretary of the navy both grew in their confidence and in their ability to handle their offices. They were the right men at the right time.

Unfortunately, the Union commander of the navy yard, Commodore (an informal rank just above captain, as the U.S. navy had no admirals at the time) C. S. McCauley was the wrong man at the wrong time. McCauley, a veteran of some 40 years of service, was quite indecisive. Claiming that he wanted to avoid provoking the Virginians, McCauley was taking no action at all to protect his yard, or the ships in it. Welles sent two other officers to try to remedy the situation. Welles dispatched the navy's chief engineer to get the *Merrimack* ready to sail. The second officer was sent to take command of the ship and, if evacuation of Norfolk was necessary, to bring the ship to Philadelphia.

On April 17, the *Merrimack* was ready to leave but McCauley refused to let the ship depart. He seemed determined to take no action at all himself and to keep others from taking action. On April 20, not knowing that Welles

The U.S.S. *Pennsylvania* was intentionally burned as part of the destruction of the Gosport Navy Yard, April 20, 1861, to keep the ships and equipment from falling into Confederate hands.

had already dispatched a regiment of army troops to try to hold the navy yard, McCauley totally lost his cool, to use a modern phrase, and ordered the Union warships in the navy yard sunk. Welles had forgotten to notify McCauley of the relief effort. A few hours later, the Union relief force arrived. Despite having enough men to hold Norfolk, the relief force commander, Hiram Paulding, compounded McCauley's error by ordering the yard blown up. Adding further insult to injury, the job was botched. The noise and light was impressive, but little was actually destroyed. Fortunately for the North, when Paulding appears again later in this story he will show far better judgment.

When the Confederates marched in a few hours later, still over a month before the Virginia electorate voted to ratify the secession decision, they found a mess but little real damage. They were able to recover most of the cannons, including 300 very state-of-the-art guns. Most importantly, the U.S.S. *Merrimack* was only partly destroyed. It had burned, but the hull and machinery were protected by the ship's having sunk to the bottom of the Elizabeth River, thereby extinguishing the fires.

A nineteenth-century historian later vividly described what the Confederates found when they entered the yard.

> Though a few shops and houses were burnt, the work was done so hurriedly that the best part of the valuable material at the yard fell into the hands of the enemy. The dry-dock was not destroyed. . . . The magazine, with great numbers of loaded shells, and 150 tons of powder [also fell into Confederate hands undamaged]. Two thousand guns of all descriptions were left practically uninjured, 300 of them being new . . . guns of various calibers. Besides the guns, machinery, steel plates, castings, construction materials, and ordnance [weapons] and equipment stores in vast quantities came into the possession of the Confederates; and severe as the loss of so much material would have been by itself to the Federal government, it was rendered tenfold greater by supplying the necessities of the enemy.[3]

The Birth of
the C.S.S. *Virginia*

The C.S.S. *Virginia* is depicted during the final stages of conversion to ironclad, with armor plate attached and adjusted. The scene shown here is probably in late February or early March 1862. The workmen would have been rushing to install the final armor plates. Some were still working when the ship steamed out on March 8, 1862, for its first combat, and they had to jump onto the dock.

The Confederates knew they had done well when they marched into the Gosport Navy Yard. The April 22, 1861, *Richmond Daily Inquirer* confidently announced that in Gosport the South now had "material enough to build a Navy of iron-plated ships."[4]

Iron-plated ships were not a new idea. As far back as the eighth century, the Vikings had created a type of ironclad. When rowing their longships, they hung their partly iron shields over the sides. By the 1840s, both the British and the Americans were building ships with iron hulls, including naval ships. The iron, however, was not intended as shielding but rather as a substitute for wood in the ship's frame.

The major spur toward iron shielding for warships came as the delayed result of an 1824 invention. A French artillery officer invented the exploding shell. Before that, cannons were only able to fire iron balls. These could cause a lot of damage when properly directed at an enemy. When heated—from which we get the term "hot shot"—the cannonball could set fire to the target ship. Solid shot, however, could also harmlessly bounce off a wooden hull or bury itself in the target ship's timbers.

Exploding shells were hollow and filled with gunpowder. They would explode on or soon after contact with the target. Wooden timbers would be dangerously splintered and scattered over a wide area, potentially causing extensive damage and casualties. It took about 30 years before the new shells really showed what they could do in combat. In November 1853, soon after the start of the Crimean War, a Turkish fleet of wooden ships was completely destroyed by a Russian fleet armed with shell-firing guns.

The French were the first to fully investigate ironclad warships. In 1859, they built and put into service the *Gloire*, a wooden-hulled ship with 4.5-inch (11-centimeter) iron shielding. Later the same year, the British launched the *Warrior*, followed soon after by the *Black Prince*. These ships were made of iron, not just made with iron shielding. By 1861, both Britain and France had more ironclads under construction.

The American naval establishment did not show much interest in ironclads. One of the few public figures to recognize the possibilities of ironclads was a senator from Florida, who was also chairman of the Senate Naval Affairs Committee. This was Stephen Mallory. By April 1861, Mallory was secretary of the navy in the Confederate government.

Mallory had to build a navy from scratch—an advantage

and a disadvantage. The disadvantage was simply that Mallory lacked a navy and also the resources needed to build a navy. His Northern counterpart, Gideon Welles, had taken over a fully functioning, if somewhat obsolete and understrength, navy. Mallory particularly lacked oceangoing vessels, though the Southern states took over some coastal and river vessels from the Union government. Many Southern naval officers "went South," resigning from the U.S. navy when their states seceded and joined the Confederacy. However, those who held commands did not bring their ships with them. The captains "retired with clean hands." Some Southern officers even sailed back to the North to return their ships before going South, to join the Confederacy. This contrasted with the record of some Southerners commanding army posts in the South. They quickly surrendered their posts to state or Confederate authorities.

Mallory had more officers than ships, so he worked at getting ships. He began improving the conventional naval resources of the Confederacy, including having oceangoing vessels built abroad, primarily in Great Britain. This had to be done quietly, since the British government had declared its neutrality. Though not always enforced, British law prohibited aid to either side.

Mallory adapted the Northern Navy Department's organizational structure for the Confederacy. However, Mallory was an advanced naval thinker. He knew that the Confederacy could never compete with the North in the number of ships. His advantage was that the Confederate had no navy and naval establishment in which to have a vested interest. The Confederacy, and its secretary of the navy, could seek new and innovative solutions.

Soon after the Confederate capture of the Gosport Navy Yard, Mallory wrote to the chairman of the Confederate House of Representatives Committee on Naval

Affairs about the innovative technological solution he had in mind.

> I regard the possession of an iron-armored ship as a
> matter of the first necessity. Such a vessel at this time

An Early Ironclad Battle

On May 10, 1861, Stephen Mallory wrote to the chairman of the Confederate House of Representatives Committee on Naval Affairs on the need for the Confederacy to build ironclad vessels. In that same letter, Mallory quoted from the noted English war correspondent William Howard Russell of the *London Times* about a battle in the Crimean War fought between Britain and France on one side and Russia on the other side in the 1850s. Russell, who witnessed the fight, described how three French ironclad batteries (picture the *Monitor,* but virtually unable to move) attacked and destroyed a Russian fort in less than an hour.

Russell wrote, as quoted by Mallory,

> The floating batteries of the French opened with a magnificent crash at 9:30 A.M. and one in particular distinguished itself for the regularity, precision, and weight of its fire throughout the day.
>
> The Russians replied with alacrity, and the batteries must have been put to a severe test for the water was splashed into pillars by shot all over them.
>
> The success of the experiment (iron-cased batteries) is complete. They were anchored only 800 yards from the Russian batteries. The shot of the enemy at that short range had no effect upon them; the balls hopped back off their sides without leaving any impression save such as a pistol ball makes on the target in a shooting gallery.
>
> The shot could be heard distinctly striking the sides of the battery with a sharp smack, and then could be seen flying back, striking the water at various angles, according to the direction they took, till they dropped exhausted.

Source: United States Department of the Navy: *Official Records of the Union and Confederate Navies in the War of the Rebellion,* Washington, D.C.: Government Print Office, 1884–1927, Series II, Volume 2, pages 68–69.

could traverse the entire coast of the United States, prevent all blockades, and encounter, with fair prospect of success, their entire Navy. If to cope with them upon the sea we follow their example and build wooden ships, we shall have to construct several at one time; for one or

Stephen Mallory, Confederate secretary of the navy. As a U.S. senator from Florida before the American Civil War, Mallory was an early advocate of the development of ironclad vessels.

two ships would fall an easy prey to her comparatively numerous steam frigates. But inequality of numbers may be compensated by invulnerability; and thus not only does economy but naval success dictate the wisdom and expediency of fighting with iron against wood, without regard to first cost.[5]

On June 3, 1861, Mallory arrived at his new offices in Richmond, Virginia, after the Confederacy moved its capital from Montgomery, Alabama. That same evening, Mallory met with Confederate Naval Lieutenant John M. Brooke, a noted naval ordnance expert. Brooke told Mallory that he thought the Confederacy, despite its industrial weakness, could build its own ironclads rather than rely on having them built in Europe.

Mallory asked Brooke to come up with a basic design and cost estimates. Brooke was a good choice for this job. He was later described as being "blessed with an inventive mind tempered with a mature sense of practicality. His designs were always simple, yet sound."[6]

A few days later, Brooke came back to Mallory with his plans. Brooke proposed what is called a shallow-draft vessel. The "draft" of a ship is the depth the ship extends below the surface of the water. A shallow-draft vessel is more flexible for operations near shore, and in rivers and other inland waters. However, it can be less stable out in the deeper ocean.

Brooke's vessel would be sharply pointed at the bow (the front of the ship) and rounded at the stern (the back). The deck would be only slightly above the water line. The engine and other vital machinery would be below the water line, safe from enemy fire. The deck itself was armored. Having the deck slightly awash, slightly underwater, was expected to supply additional protection.

On top of the deck Brooke placed the combat heart of his vessel. This was a casemate. The casemate would be an

John M. Brooke was co-designer of the C.S.S. *Virginia*. During construction of the ironclad, Brooke's primary task was to obtain and ensure proper application of the armor plate. This photograph was most likely taken after the Civil War.

iron-enclosed structure, rounded at both ends, roughly 20 feet (six meters) high, covering about half the deck space. The sides would slope upward, at about a 45-degree angle, designed to increase the chance that cannonballs would just bounce off. Brooke himself later described the casemate as "a shield of timber, two feet thick, plated with three or more inches of iron, inclined to the horizontal plane at the least angle that would permit working the guns."[7] The analogy most people would use on seeing the final result was that the casemate made the vessel look like a floating barn.

Brooke called for at least three inches of iron plating on the wooden casemate. The shielding would extend several feet below the water on the left (port) and right (starboard) sides of the ship. This was supposed to allow the ship to sit higher in the water, as it used up coal and ammunition during battle, and still keep the hull invulnerable to enemy fire.

Most of the ship's cannons would be fired broadside, in set directions to either side. Ports, or openings, in the sides of the casemate, would allow the cannons to be rolled out, with their barrels through the ports, to be fired, then they would be pulled back inside to be loaded. Pivot guns, able to rotate from side to side, in the bow and stern could be fired straight ahead and to either side. Armored shutters would close when the guns were being loaded, to protect the guns and gun crews.

Brooke's design was not totally revolutionary; similar ideas had been presented in Europe 80 years before. However, no ship had actually been built with this design. Brooke was showing Mallory what would become the basic design for virtually all Confederate ironclads built during the American Civil War.

Mallory quickly approved Brooke's plans. Brooke then suggested that John L. Porter, the former chief designer of the U.S. navy, now at Gosport, and the Confederate chief naval engineer, William P. Williamson, come to Richmond to help build some ironclads from Brooke's basic design. Mallory, however, sent for what he called a "practical mechanic"[8] from Norfolk. About all this man could do was to provide some suggestions on the type of timbers to use. Mallory quickly dismissed him. On June 22, 1861, Mallory sent for Porter and Williamson.

Neither knew the purpose of the meeting when they received Mallory's call. However, Porter brought something with him. Porter had been thinking about ironclad vessels for a while, as far back as 1846, he would later claim. About

20 years later, Porter wrote "In April, 1846, I had been stationed in Pittsburg [*sic*] superintending an iron steamer, when I conceived the idea of an iron-clad, and made a model with the exact shield I placed on the *Merrimac*."[9] Porter also claimed to have sent the idea to the U.S. Navy Department a few years later, though no evidence exists of this.

When the Civil War started, Porter again started thinking about ironclads. He took into account the limitations of Southern industry, and what he saw as the primary need to use such a vessel for harbor defense. This time Porter created a model. This model looked very similar to Brooke's design and to the ultimate design, except there was no projecting bow or stern under the casemate. Porter brought the model with him to Richmond.

Mallory, Brooke, Porter, and Williamson met in Brooke's office on June 23, 1861. They started by discussing Porter's model. All four men liked Porter's casemate design. The 40-degree proposed incline would make it even harder for incoming shells to hit straight on. Brooke and Porter agreed on all features of the casemate, including the idea of having eaves with heavier shielding extending two feet (half a meter) below the waterline. A casemate almost exactly like the one proposed by Porter, and not that far from the one Brooke had proposed, was adopted.

The primary difference in Brooke's design was that the bow and stern decks projected beyond the shield. These decks, designed to be submerged, eventually extended 29 feet (9 meters) in front, 55 feet (17 meters) to the rear. Porter was told to prepare new structural plans for the ship. Brooke and Williamson were dispatched to Norfolk to see about needed engines and other machinery.

Before leaving they went to the Tredegar Iron Works in Richmond, the primary iron foundry in the South. The Tredegar staff gave them bad news. The South did not have engines like the ones they wanted. A day or two later, Brooke and Williamson met with Porter to discuss this problem. Williamson remarked, talking about the proposed ironclad, that "It will take at least 12 months to build her engines unless we can utilize some of the machinery in the *Merrimac*."[10] They quickly came to the conclusion that they might be able to use more than just the engines from the *Merrimack*. The *Merrimack* had burned to the waterline when the Union evacuated Gosport. However, the water put out the fire, leaving the hull and the engines wet but otherwise undamaged.

Records are unclear as to who first made the suggestion to build the ironclad on the remains of the *Merrimack*. However, the three engineers quickly realized that their ironclad design only needed a little adaptation to be built using the hull of that ship. They reported to Mallory that the *Merrimack* could be adapted to an ironclad with four guns on each side, one each in the bow and stern. They estimated it would cost about $110,000 total, a total that later increased but stayed under $200,000.

Mallory approved the revised plans. Porter went back to Gosport to plan the conversion. He first literally measured the ship by hand. He then calculated the weight of the *Merrimack*'s components to find out how much additional weight it could carry. Porter came up with the interesting conclusion that the result would be about 50 tons too light to keep the shielding properly under water. It may seem strange to read that a ship is too light. However, ships need to have a proper balance of weight, even when the designers are not worried about unshielded hulls becoming visible above the waterline, and vulnerable to enemy fire. A ship that is too heavy might sink. A ship that rides too high in the waters in which it is designed to operate may not be stable.

Porter changed the design of the propeller. Mallory then

held a conference on July 11 with Porter, Brooke, and Williamson and the plans were approved. Mallory issued an order to the Confederate commandant of the Gosport Navy Yard to proceed immediately with building the ironclad.

The *Merrimack* has been brought out of the water six weeks before. At first glance, the ship was a mess. The few timbers remaining above the waterline looked like, and actually were, giant pieces of burnt charcoal. The decking was destroyed, as was the smokestack. Brass parts were twisted, and when the ship was brought out of the water, every iron part began to rust immediately. Acting Chief Engineer H. Ashton Ramsay, who would serve on the new ironclad in its most famous action, later wrote, "when she was raised by the Confederates she was nothing but a burned and blackened hulk."[11]

The commander of the Union blockade squadron that included the Norfolk area agreed with the negative assessments, as he told Gideon Welles in a letter. Union opinion would change as they received reports of Confederate progress at recycling the *Merrimack*. Recycling was not a term they would have used in 1861, but it does describe what the Confederates were doing. The South had a substantially weaker industrial base than the North. It had to reuse, to recycle, whatever it could.

Mallory did not agree with the negative Union assessments. In July 1861, after telling Porter, Brooke, and Williamson to start work, Mallory asked the Confederate Congress for an appropriation of $172,523, which he received.

Work had already begun. Infighting among the three primary creators also began. Porter was put in charge of the entire project. Brooke was in charge of the armor and weapons, but he was also Mallory's representative on the project team. Williamson was in charge of the engines and other machinery. Brooke and Porter began to dispute credit for the design, an argument never fully settled

Line engraving published in *Harper's Weekly* (currently *Harper's*) in 1861. The engraving shows the U.S.S. *Merrimack* (incorrectly but usually spelled *Merrimac*) under repair at the Gosport Navy Yard, early 1861.

between them. Fortunately, from the Confederate point of view, their disputes had little impact on the progress of the work.

REBUILDING THE *MERRIMACK*

The first task was to clean away the unusable portions of the old *Merrimack*. Basically, everything three feet (one meter) above the waterline was cut away. The gun deck was placed on this surface. At the end of July, with the gun deck complete, Porter's men began building the casemate. Mallory was calling for a hectic pace. Almost 1,500 men worked on the ship, sometimes working Sundays and nights—Saturday was a regular part of the workweek. The effort was making progress, but two problems were arising.

The *Merrimack*'s engines were not considered reliable.

In fact, the ship had been awaiting engine replacement when the Gosport Navy Yard fell to the Confederates. Acting Chief Engineer Ramsay had served on the *Merrimack*. During one two-year cruise, he later wrote, the ship had to use its sails most of the time. He had been sent to assist Williamson in getting the engines running. Ramsay knew he had to find ways to keep the balky engines running at all times, because the new ironclad would not have sails.

Brooke was in charge of finding the armor and guns for the ironclad. Brooke seems to have worked very hard at his job. An associate wrote, "He is an indefatigable fellow and works with head and heart for our glorious cause."[12] Brooke began, in late July, by contracting with the Tredegar Iron Works to supply one-inch-thick (2.5-centimeter-thick) iron plate, eight inches (20 centimeters) wide, in different lengths. He also had to arrange the supply of most of the iron itself used in the plates. His major source of iron was scrap iron, from wrecked equipment at the Gosport yard and from used railroad rails.

Brooke got his one-inch (2.5-centimeter) iron plate. He soon thought, however, that the initial intention to have a total of three inches (eight centimeters) of armor might not be sufficient. Tredegar was now asked to make plate two inches (5 centimeters) thick, for a total of four inches (10 centimeters) of armor on the vessel. This created problems. The plate needed holes for the bolts to attach it to the wooden backing. One-inch plate could be punched. Two-inch plate had to be drilled. Design changes made the cost of the iron plates go up.

Mallory ordered Brooke to conduct tests on the iron armor. Brooke went to Jamestown in October to meet with the commander of the Confederate batteries in the area, Confederate Navy Lieutenant Thomas Catesby ap Roger Jones. (*Ap* is Welsh, meaning "son of.") The tests Brooke and Jones carried out found that three-inch armor would not prevent solid cannonballs from penetrating the wood backing. Four inches of iron worked, however. The cannonball penetrated the first two-inch layer but only cracked the second layer. The wood was not penetrated at all. A third test, using iron rails, proved that four-inch armor was the best of the three possibilities. Tredegar was able to produce sufficient quantities of the two-inch iron plates Brooke needed.

That same October, the Confederates realized that word of progress on the *Merrimack* was leaking to the Union. The Navy Department leaked a false story that the tests on the *Merrimack*'s armor proved that the armor was worthless. There is no indication that Welles and the Union navy paid attention to these reports.

Brooke had selected the guns for the ship even before the armor problem was settled. He designed a seven-inch (18-centimeter) gun (firing a projectile seven inches in diameter) for the ship. Two of these guns would be used, along with six nine-inch (23-centimeter) guns and two 6.5-inch (16.5-centimeter) pivot guns, one in the bow (the front of the ship), and one in the stern (the back of the ship) that could rotate from side to side as well as be moved back and forth.

In early November, Lieutenant Jones was relieved of his duties at Jamestown and appointed executive officer of the new ironclad. He was charged with testing the guns, speeding up construction of the ship, and obtaining a crew. The latter presented some problems. Jones had no problem getting officers. Getting enlisted men, however, was more difficult. Most enlisted men in the pre–Civil War "old navy" had been from the North. Jones got help from Lieutenant John Taylor Wood, assigned to the *Merrimack* in January 1862. Wood obtained some experienced seamen from Norfolk. Others came from New Orleans army units, including men with seafaring backgrounds, serving in the Norfolk area. However, some gunners without nautical experience had to be recruited from the Confederate army.

A final military feature of the *Merrimack* was added almost at the last minute. Porter, at the insistence of the Navy Department, and of Mallory himself, added a 1,500-pound (680-kilogram) iron ram to the front of the ship, reviving something not seen on warships for hundreds of years. Rams enable ships to slam into the side of enemy ships, with relative safety, with the intent of punching a hole large enough to sink the enemy. Ships powered by banks of oars had precise enough control over speed and direction to hit an enemy ship, a relatively small target. Sailing ships, though far more efficiently propelled, lacked the precise control and could not be used as rams. Mallory and his department figured that a steam-powered iron warship could safely revive ramming. However, the ram was not well installed. One of the connecting mounts was cracked during installation and nothing was done to fix it.

A far more serious error was Porter's miscalculation of the weight of the vessel. On February 17, 1862, the ship was launched and commissioned as the C.S.S. *Virginia*. The designers then discovered that the ship was too light. The decks were not even slightly underwater. Even worse, the eaves from the casemate shielding were also barely underwater. Several hundred tons of pig iron was added as ballast, designed to give more weight to the ship. Ammunition and coal would add further weight to the vessel. However, the shielded eaves would still be only a few inches underwater. This would remain a major weakness.

The Union leadership had a good idea of what was going on with the *Merrimack*, now called the *Virginia*. And they were not standing idle.

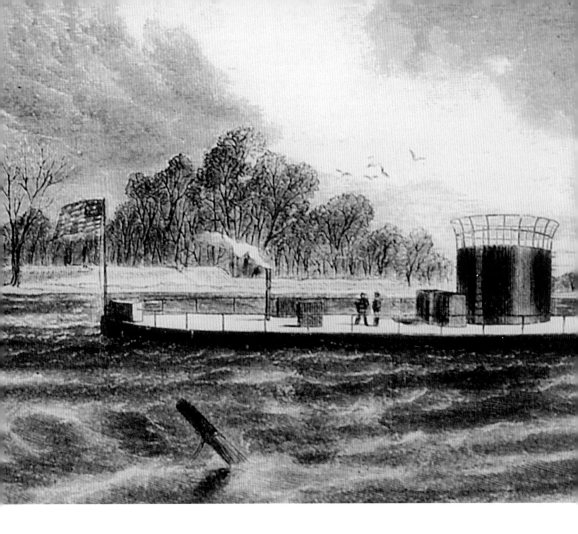

The Birth of the
U.S.S. *Monitor*

3

Engraving of the U.S.S. *Monitor*, published in *Harper's Weekly*, March 22, 1862, about two weeks after its battle with the C.S.S. *Virginia*. The turret is shown too tall in proportion to the rest of the ship. Surprisingly, no photos are known to exist of the entire U.S.S. *Monitor* or any part of the C.S.S. *Virginia*.

G ideon Welles, Union secretary of the navy, faced a different problem from Stephen Mallory's. Mallory had to create a navy from scratch, with few economic and industrial resources to do it. Welles had a navy, but one that was far inadequate for its task. Forty-two warships on active duty, though mostly up to date, even had many not been spread out to the far corners of the world, could not even approach creating a successful blockade of some 3,000 miles (4,828 kilometers) of Southern coastline. His navy did come with an entrenched bureaucracy, long-established officers and civilian personnel with the potential to block innovation. Welles also had to build a navy.

Welles did not have Stephen Mallory's extensive naval experience.

Welles, however, had worked in the Navy Department from about 1845–1847, serving as chief of the Bureau of Provisions and Clothing. This was not exactly a place for strategic, tactical, or technical innovation, but it did give him some background for his difficult task.

Welles, when he took office, lacked Mallory's enthusiasm for ironclad vessels. But he also had few preconceptions. Despite early reports of Confederate plans, Welles's senior subordinates were skeptical about ironclads. Welles was a little more impressed with the reports, and with the fact that the U.S. army was already building ironclads for use on western rivers. In early July 1861, almost as an afterthought to other legislation, Welles asked Congress for $1.5 million for the construction of three prototype ironclads. The legislation called for Welles to appoint a three-member board to consider and select designs for further development.

On August 3, 1861, the ironclad bill was passed by Congress and signed by President Lincoln. On August 7, Welles issued an advertisement asking people to submit designs within a few weeks. The next day, he choose three senior naval officers for his board—Commodore Joseph Smith, Commodore Hiram Paulding (the same officer who had ordered the destruction of the Gosport Navy Yard), and Captain Charles H. Davis.

Seventeen proposed designs soon arrived. The board found two of these designs to have potential for further study and development. One was a steam frigate, a conventional ship of the time with sails and a motor, but it also had armor. This design would be built, at a projected cost of $780,000, as the U.S.S. *New Ironsides*. The second was another relatively conventional design, with armor attached to the sides "much like the clapboard siding on a house."[13] This ship, at a proposed cost of $235,000, would eventually become the U.S.S. *Galena*.

This design also had an unexpected result. The ship had

been proposed by C.S. Bushnell and Company of New Haven, Connecticut. The board had one concern and it requested an answer from Bushnell. The board thought the ship would be too heavy, float too low at sea, and not be stable. Bushnell spoke with a New York iron maker he knew, also in Washington. This iron maker suggested that Bushnell go to New York and speak with John Ericsson, an accomplished but controversial ship designer and inventor originally from Sweden.

Fifty-eight years old, born in Sweden, Captain Ericsson (his title being the rank earned from service in the Swedish army) had moved to London in 1826. While in Great Britain he invented a railroad engine and a fire engine. He developed the first screw propeller, an underwater propeller for moving ships. Steamships at the time used large wooden paddle wheels on the side or rear. These took up a lot of room on commercial vessels. On warships, they made very attractive targets for an attacking enemy. The screw propeller would be underwater, as would most of the engine operating the propeller. It is here that Ericsson began thinking about a partially submerged warship.

There was little interest in Great Britain in his design. So in 1839, Ericsson moved to New York, at the urging of an American naval officer named Robert F. Stockton. By 1842, the politically influential Stockton had arranged for Ericsson to get the contract for a navy ship, the U.S.S. *Princeton*. The most innovative feature of the *Princeton* was that its most important parts—its engine (also designed by Ericsson) and its propeller—were underwater.

However, the vessel might have been a bit too innovative. Ericsson designed a cannon for the ship. This gun could fire a 225-pound (102-kilogram) projectile five miles (eight kilometers), with accuracy, making it one of the best naval cannons in the world. Ericsson protected the breach, the back of the gun where the gunpowder is actually

(continued on page 42)

H.M.S. *Warrior*

A side from the C.S.S. *Virginia,* commissioned a week before the U.S.S. *Monitor*, probably the most famous ironclad predecessor to the Union ironclad was the British ship H.M.S. *Warrior.* The *Warrior*'s construction and launch was a direct and immediate result of the launch, a year before, of the French ironclad *Gloire,* and France's plans for further similar warships. The French ship was a standard warship of the day, powered by sail and engines, but with iron plating over wooden sides and deck. However, the continuing military rivalry between Britain and France sparked a demand by the British government for a response surpassing the French effort.

The H.M.S. *Warrior,* and its sister ship the H.M.S. *Black Prince,* were Britain's response. The *Warrior* was ordered on June 1859 and launched on December 29, 1860. It froze to the shipway on a very cold day. Several tugs pulled the ship, while several hundred men ran from side to side on the deck to rock it loose. After about half an hour, the ship finally entered the water.

The *Warrior* had several innovative features, besides the iron armor. The hull was built of iron. It had watertight compartments inside, designed to try to minimize damage from any water that might enter the ship. It was also the largest warship yet built, 410 feet (125 meters) longer than the *Virginia* and roughly twice the size of the *Monitor*. The *Warrior*'s guns were arranged in broadsides, like the *Virginia*'s, following standard practice of that time. Each broadside had 24 guns, rivaling that of the Confederate ironclad. The *Warrior* also had an interesting innovation for the comfort of the crew, easily dirtied by the large amount of coal the ship required to operate. The *Warrior* was the first warship to have built-in washing machines.

H.M.S. *Warrior* was a very impressive ship for the time. It and the H.M.S. *Black Prince* were superior to their French rivals. However, the *Warrior* never saw action. The Battle of Hampton Roads convinced the British admiralty that turreted warships were the wave of the future. By 1883, the *Warrior* had been retired from sea service, to serve for close to the next century as a supply hulk—basically a floating warehouse. The *Warrior* still exists today, the only one of the 45 iron-hulled British warships built between 1861 and 1877 to survive, and is being restored to its original condition.

H.M.S. Warrior, *the first British ironclad, shown during an 1872–1875 refit. Though it was commissioned about a year before the U.S.S.* Monitor *and C.S.S.* Virginia, *the H.M.S.* Warrior *was a conventionally designed vessel made of iron instead of wood.*

(continued from page 39)

ignited, with a heavy metal band. Stockton created a variation to Ericsson's gun, but without the breach protection. Stockton was demonstrating his gun when it blew up, killing the U.S. secretary of state, the secretary of the navy, and the father of President John Tyler's fiancée. Tyler and his fiancée had planned to watch the demonstration but were delayed below deck.

Stockton managed to shift the blame to Ericsson, and saw to it that Ericsson was never paid for his work. An interesting historical irony is that one of Ericsson's few supporters in Washington was the senator from Florida, Stephen Mallory. Ericsson was the stereotypical creative genius, frequently very hard to work with, so the navy personnel were likely quite happy to see Ericsson blamed for the disaster and to not deal with him further. This whole experience gave him a strong dislike of the U.S. navy.

Ericsson, however, was a strong supporter of the Union government and very proud that, since 1848, he had been an American citizen. He was happy to help Bushnell—doing a few calculations and then informing Bushnell that his ship would be stable at sea. Ericsson then asked a question. As Bushnell later remembered, "Captain Ericsson asked if I had time just then to examine the plan of a floating battery absolutely impregnable to the heaviest shot or shell."[14] Bushnell agreed.

Ericsson's design had been developed in 1854 and sent to Napoleon III of France. All Ericsson got for his efforts was a polite rejection letter from a French naval official. The design had a hemisphere-shaped rotating gun turret in the middle of a two-part hull. The guns were supposed to be steam-powered, and breach-loading, where the shells are loaded in the back of the gun. This was a more efficient way of loading and firing artillery ammunition, though a breach-loading gun was harder to design and build.

The upper hull was armored, with substantial overhang above the lower hull. The ship would have to be deeply penetrated by a ramming vessel before suffering any real damage. The only other structure above deck was a small pilothouse. The anchor well was completely protected by armor. The engines, like the propeller and the rudder for navigation, were underwater. Crew quarters were also underwater. Ericsson developed a ventilation system for the crew quarters and engine room. With conventional guns and a few other minor changes, this vessel became the U.S.S. *Monitor.*

Surprisingly, very little about Ericsson's design was totally new. Even the screw propeller and the idea of the engines below the waterline had been used before—though in this case Ericsson was using his own ideas. What was innovative was putting a whole collection of these ideas together in one vessel.

Ericsson had a deserved reputation for being temperamental. However, he could also be charming and eloquent when talking about one of his many inventions. He kept Bushnell's attention while he described his ironclad. Ericsson explained that his ship would be able to operate in narrow channels, a major advantage. The revolving turret meant the ship did not have to be maneuvered to aim the guns. Due to its relatively shallow draft (how deep the ship sits in water) it could operate in shallow coastal waters, such as Hampton Roads. Perhaps most importantly, Ericsson said, the ship could be built quickly.

Bushnell asked Ericsson if he would submit the design to Welles. Ericsson agreed, despite his poor relations with the navy. Bushnell went to see Welles, who was in Hartford, Connecticut, arranging his family's move down to Washington. Welles liked the idea and asked Bushnell to take the idea to the ironclad board in Washington. Bushnell decided on a stop, first, that might make it easier to deal

John Ericsson, designer of the U.S.S. *Monitor,* photographed in 1862.

with Union bureaucracy. He stopped in Troy, New York, to speak with his two partners on the *Galena* ironclad project, John A. Griswold and John F. Winslow. They helped him get a letter from Secretary of State William Seward to President Lincoln.

The next day, September 12, 1861, Bushnell met with President Lincoln. Lincoln was impressed with Bushnell's idea and agreed to accompany Bushnell on September 13 to present the idea to the board. On that day, Bushnell and Lincoln, met with Commodores Smith and Paulding from the board and Assistant Secretary of the Navy Gustavus Fox. Captain Davis was absent. Smith and Paulding agreed to endorse the plan if Davis agreed. At a meeting of the entire board the next day, September 14, which the president did not attend, Davis did not agree. A simple "no" was apparently not sufficient for Davis. Instead, he told Bushnell to "Take that little thing home and worship it, as it would not be idolatry, because it is in the image of nothing in the heaven above or on the earth beneath or in the waters under the earth." [15]

Bushnell did not take no, not even Davis's elaborately insulting version of no, for an answer. Bushnell, just the day before, had seen how charming and persuasive Ericsson could be when speaking in support of his own inventions. Bushnell, therefore, first had Welles arrange a meeting between Ericsson and the board in Welles's office. Bushnell then spent the night on a train back to New York. He told Ericsson that Smith and Paulding supported the idea, which was true. He then told Ericsson that Davis had a few questions, which Ericsson himself would have to answer.

Ericsson nearly walked out of the meeting in Washington the next day when he found out that his visit was unexpected and unwelcome. When finally told that his plan had already been rejected, Ericsson asked why. Smith said they thought the ironclad would not be stable enough. Ericsson then explained why Smith was wrong, and why his ship was worth building. Bushnell later wrote to Welles that Ericsson "thrilled every person in your room with his vivid description of what the little boat would be and what she could do."[16] Most importantly, he told the board he could build the ship in three months. By the end of the day, Ericsson received approval for his vessel.

Ericsson immediately returned to New York to start work. In modern terms, he decided to subcontract his project. The hull would be built at Greenpoint, Brooklyn, by the Thomas F. Rowland Continental Iron Works, for a price of 7.5 cents per pound. The turret would be constructed across the East River in New York City (Brooklyn did not become part of New York City until 1895) by the Novelty Iron Works. The same iron maker who referred Bushnell to Ericsson and got the whole process started would build the engines. Several other iron mills would produce the armor.

Ericsson's partners took an interesting action at this time. In 1843, a man named Theodore Timby in Upstate New York had developed a type of revolving turret and constructed a model. President John Tyler examined the model. However, two years later, a military commission recommended against further investigation of the idea. Timby also had not finished the patent application process. The partners, although, wanted to use the turret design and decided to pay Timby a $5,000 royalty on every turreted ship they might build. They thought this would keep Timby from disputing the unapproved use in court.

Ericsson did not have a contract yet and he needed money to advance to the contractors. Winslow, Griswold, and Bushnell each advanced money for a quarter share of the profits. All of this was taking place just about six weeks after the Welles's original "request for proposals" in August 1861.

Ericsson's contract arrived a few days later. Some resistance had arisen in Washington to the innovative new design, and to Ericsson himself. Speed requirements were set for the ship. Ericsson had to provide spars, masts, and

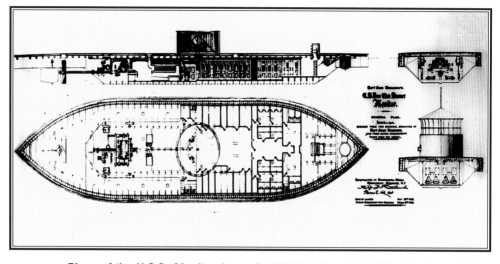

Plans of the U.S.S. *Monitor* drawn in 1862 by the staff of the Continental Iron Works, Brooklyn, where the ship was built.

sails, despite the fact that sail power was impossible in the design. Sails would have destroyed the stability of the ship and would have also interfered with the use of the turret. Ericsson ignored this requirement. Ericsson had just 90 days to build his ship. He would be paid $275,000 in biweekly installments subject to approval by the Navy Department. Finally, 25 percent payment would be held back until the ship was proven. The contract also required the ship to be a complete success, or the government would get its money back. The ship's first test, which won its approval, would be the battle with the *Virginia*. So, the Union government did not even fully own the warship when it went into combat.

BUILDING THE *MONITOR*

Another possible problem was the appointment of the Navy Department's representative to the project. This representative would be the one to certify progress and to pay Ericsson and his associates. He would have to work with

Ericsson, a man an acquaintance described as "a high-pressure steam engine himself."[17] Chief Engineer Alban C. Stimers, 34 years old, was chosen. (Chief engineer was a job title; Stimers was not the chief engineer of the entire navy.) Stimers was an expert on steam engines. He was not popular with his associates in the navy, and was considered to have an arrogant personality to go with his fast promotion and talent. Stimers was much like Ericsson and they quickly became close friends. Stimers became one of Ericsson's strongest supporters.

The ship's keel was laid on October 25, 1861. With round-the-clock effort, it took just a few weeks for the ship's hull to be ready to receive the various subcontracted parts. Ericsson was saving valuable time with his subcontracting. He also was finding that his initial plans had been so good that the various parts of the ship fit together with little adjustment. One possible problem emerged, though. Ericsson had designed his ship with blowers to force air into the boiler system. With the ship's low freeboard—the distance between the deck and the water—the openings for the blowers might also allow water to get into the system. This could stop the blowers and force deadly carbon monoxide into the boiler room and then into the entire vessel.

The second key part of the ship was the turret. The turret would sit on giant ball bearings, resting on a huge brass ring on the deck of the ship. The final arrangement was designed to remain watertight, while still being able to rotate. The turret was 9 feet (3 meters) high, 20 feet (6 meters) across inside—very crowded with a full gun crew and the two 11-inch (28-centimeter) guns. It was also very heavy, too heavy to ship across the river to Brooklyn. The turret was taken apart and reassembled on the ship's deck.

By this point, January 1862, skeptics still thought little of the ship. Welles and Commodore Smith, however, still remained supportive. They began looking for someone to command the ship. Command was offered to Lieutenant John Lorimer Worden, a native of Sing-Sing, New York, about 75 miles (121 kilometers) up the Hudson River from New York City. Worden had been a Confederate prisoner until November 1861, having been captured on the way back from delivering orders to a Union fort in Florida. Worden accepted the offer, and on January 16, 1862, formally took over command.

"Ericsson's ship" or "Ericsson's folly" were not particularly catchy names for a warship. Assistant Navy Secretary Fox asked Ericsson to suggest a name. Ericsson replied that the ship would provide a monitor to the leaders of the Southern rebellion and to foreign leaders who might consider intervening. The name U.S.S. *Monitor* entered naval history.

However, the *Monitor* was late in entering history. Ericsson's contracted delivery date was January 12, 1862. Welles dropped his idea to sail the *Monitor* to Hampton Roads, then to Gosport Navy Yard to destroy the place and the Confederate ironclad with gunfire. Welles thought the ship could have accomplished this task with little difficulty.

Worden now had to select a crew. The key members of the 57-man crew were Executive Officer Lieutenant Samuel Dana Greene, an engineer named Isaac Newton, and Paymaster William Keeler. Alban Stimers, though not formally a member of the crew, would sail with the ship and serve as chief engineer.

By February 19, the *Monitor* was officially turned over to the navy. Due to an error in setting steam valves, the *Monitor* could only move very slowly. It took over five hours to steam to the Brooklyn Navy Yard. This problem was easily corrected later, however. On February 25, 1862, the U.S.S. *Monitor* was commissioned. Two days later, the ship was fully loaded and headed south. Worden soon discovered problems with the steering, however. The ship ran back and forth between Brooklyn and Manhattan, until it finally banged into the New York gasworks. The *Monitor* had to be towed back to the Brooklyn Navy Yard.

By March 6, the *Monitor* was finally ready, and the

Blockades

Despite all of the trouble carrying out the strategy, despite all of the false starts, and despite all of the bloodshed the strategy cost, the overall and eventually successful Union strategy for winning the American Civil War was determined at the start of the war. A key part of this strategy was to seal off the South's 3,000 miles (4,828 kilometers) of coastline and close its ports to all foreign commerce and possible military assistance. Abraham Lincoln and his administration did this because they were well aware of the vital role outside assistance had played in winning the American Revolution.

The first problem the North faced was what to call its seacoast effort. "Closing ports" is something a nation does on its own territory. The Lincoln administration considered this option because it would avoid giving the South even an implied recognition as an independent state. However, a government that has closed some of its ports does not have the right to stop and search neutral vessels. Had the Lincoln administration tried to merely "close the ports" of the South and stop neutral vessels to enforce the closure, this could have created major diplomatic problems.

Formally proclaiming a blockade would allow stopping neutral ships, but this created other problems. One can only legally blockade a foreign government, and this would imply the Confederacy was an independent foreign government rather than an organized domestic revolt. The second problem was that a blockade had to be effective in order to be legal. International law and treaties interpreted this to mean not that the blockade had to catch every vessel trying to get through, but that these vessels had to be running a real risk of being caught, searched, and possibly seized.

The Union blockade of Southern ports was never fully effective. There was, however, increasing risk to blockade runners of getting caught. Therefore, the blockade proved increasingly effective as a tool of Union strategy.

weather was good for departure. At 4:00 P.M. it got under way. Three other vessels—*Sachem*, *Currituck*, and *Seth Low*—accompanied the *Monitor*. The *Monitor*'s departure was well timed. Worden missed new orders from Welles, sending the ship to Washington, D.C., rather than to Hampton Roads.

Statue of John Ericsson in Battery Park in lower Manhattan, New York City. The statue stands about 75 yards (69 meters) from the tip of Manhattan. Created by Johnathan Scott Hartley, the statue was dedicated on April 26, 1893. The inscription on the pedestal reads, "The City of New York erects this statue to the memory of a citizen whose genius has contributed to the greatness of the republic and the progress of the world."

Getting to War

The first 25 miles (40 kilometers) or so of the *Monitor*'s voyage took it from the Brooklyn Navy Yard, down the East River, through New York Harbor, past Staten Island, to Sandy Hook, New Jersey. Sandy Hook, a hook-shaped peninsula stretching east and then curving north, visible from the tip of Staten Island, marked the entrance to the Atlantic Ocean. Towed by the steamer *Seth Low*, and using its own engines as well, the *Monitor* was making about four knots, very roughly five miles (eight kilometers) per hour. This part of the voyage took about five hours. Most of the crew was working below decks, or simply "below," as sailors say. The ship's few portholes were green glass discs inserted in the ceiling to provide natural light during the day. The crewmen were unable to enjoy the scenery.

A ship leaving New York Harbor will sail south, then almost directly east for a short period, regardless of its ultimate destination. This was true of the *Monitor*. Once it passed Sandy Hook and entered the Atlantic Ocean, the *Monitor* and the accompanying ships swung south. Fortunately, the frequently temperamental north Atlantic Ocean, known for the suddenness and ferocity of its storms, was behaving, at least for the first 12 hours or so of the voyage. The ship itself almost sat on top of the waves, with little water splashing on deck. When night fell, soon after entering the Atlantic, the escorts could be seen in the bright moonlight a short distance to the east. The *Seth Low* was visible 400 yards (366 meters) ahead, connected to the *Monitor* by a thick tow-rope. In the further distance, sailing ships with white sails going in various directions were visible on all sides.

The *Monitor* was new to its men as well as to the navy. Laborers had been working on the ship almost until the moment of departure, and the crew did not have time to get to know the ship. The men took time to acquaint themselves with the guns and engines, and with the innovative turret and blower system supplying air to the boilers. The boilers, providing steam to run the engines, were just below and in back of the chamber below the turret. Watertight bulkheads, the naval term for walls, effectively sealed off the boiler chamber from the turret chamber. They were designed not just to protect the ship from flooding, but also to provide an airtight seal for the boiler room in order to make the engines work more efficiently and to prevent smoke and gas from the fires from spreading into the rest of the ship.

The boilers worked by forced air brought in by blowers from two openings in the deck. Any air that leaked out made the engines run less efficiently. The blowers also forced air up through the smokestacks. Normally level with the deck, temporary six-foot (two-meter) stacks had been mounted for the voyage. The danger came from the air intakes sitting less than two feet (half a meter) above the water. Water could easily come directly into the blowers and knock off their powering drive belts, decreasing the intake of air. More dangerously, smoke and carbon monoxide could leak into the rest of the ship. If the crewmen did not react quickly, this could kill them.

The crew found another Ericsson invention, a flush toilet. On sailing ships, waste products were dumped over the side, but this was not possible with a ship virtually underwater. Ericsson found a solution. One valve closed the toilet off from the ship; a second opened it to the sea. A pump then forced the waste products out into the ocean. "Essentially the same system for evacuating waste was in use in submarines during the Second World War."[18]

Unfortunately for the North, yet another Ericsson innovation included in the original plans for the *Monitor* could not be developed in the rush to build the boat. Two underwater tubes, one on each side of the vessel, would fire "hydrostatic javelins" powered by steam. The javelins were ten feet (three meters) long with explosive warheads. When this idea was developed some years later and given the name used in the Civil War for explosive mines, they became the murderously effective primary weapon of submarines — torpedoes.

Experienced sailors would have been used to crowded conditions and to sleeping on hammocks. They might have been a bit taken aback when they realized that an iron vessel reflected and magnified outside temperatures. It has to have been a shock to wake at 5:00 A.M. in a room with temperatures barely above freezing.

The officers were more comfortable. For one thing, noise coming through the thin interior walls awakened them at 5:00 A.M. with the enlisted men, the officers could at least go back to sleep for another three hours. William Keeler's cabin was typical of the other officers' rooms, except for the captain, who had more luxurious quarters. Keeler's floor was covered with an oilcloth, which helped keep it dry. A rug covered the oilcloth, with a soft mat on top of that. The woodwork was polished black walnut with brass railings and fixtures. Keeler's cabin included storage closets along the wall and drawers under his bunk, or berth. One shelf held a washbasin with another for drinking water, soap, and other needed supplies. The floor had an opening for ventilation from the blower system. Still, the room was sufficiently crowded that there was no room for some books Keeler had brought with him. He had to keep them on his bed during the day and move them onto the floor at night.

The officers were not quite as cold as the men. The wardroom, in the center of the officers' cabins, had steam heaters installed before the *Monitor* left New York. This warmed up the cabins somewhat. Still, Keeler "made the discovery that there are some things about [life on a warship] not very romantic."[19]

The night of March 6 passed peacefully, if a bit cold, for the crew of the *Monitor*. At the least, the ocean was calm, but this began to change early the next morning. The wind began to pick up, blowing in from the west. Waves started to break over the deck making it dangerous for the men. Alban Stimers later wrote that "the sea commenced to wash right across the deck, but if there were no bulwarks to keep the water off, so also there were none to keep in on . . . our lee side [the side away from the wind, in this case the left, or port, side] was a regular Niagara Falls."[20] There also would have been nothing to keep any man caught on deck from being swept over the side.

A safety precaution, one taken without Ericsson's authorization, began to cause problems. Ericsson had designed the turret to make a watertight seal with the upper deck of

The officers of the U.S.S. *Monitor* in July 1862. The major figures in the battle shown are Paymaster William Keeler, (second from right, top row), Engineer Isaac Newton (furthest to right, top row), and Lieutenant Samuel Dana Greene (furthest to left, middle row).

the ship. However, before the *Monitor* left the Brooklyn Navy Yard, someone had ordered the turret jacked up a few inches and a thick rope inserted between the bottom of the turret and the brass ring. Unfortunately, this did not work. The water was steadily dripping through the space between the turret and the deck. By morning, other leaks had sprung up. The men were driven from their hammocks in a vain attempt to find a dry place to sleep.

Samuel Dana Greene, executive officer (second in command) of the *Monitor*, described the worsening situation. The water "would strike the pilothouse and go over the turret in beautiful curves, and it came through the narrow eye-holes in the pilothouse with such force as to knock the helmsman completely round from the wheel."[21] The ride was so rough that some crewmembers were becoming unbearably seasick, including the captain and the ship's surgeon. These crewmembers were taken to the top of the turret to at least get some fresh air, though one doubts that they were able to stay dry.

At 4:00 P.M. the rough seas stopped being just annoying. Paymaster Keeler started to go below when he ran into Alban Stimers, one of the engineers, coming up. Stimers was coated black with smoke and barely able to speak or breathe. Keeler went below to get Stimers some brandy, used as a medicinal stimulant at the time. Almost immediately, Keeler ran into some sailors bringing up a fireman (one of the crewmen assigned to keep the fires fed with fuel) and the other three engineers. All four looked dead to Keeler. They almost were, having barely escaped the lower deck where the engines were located.

The *Monitor* had a major problem: Its ventilation system had broken down. Ocean water coming through the blower vents on deck had loosened the drive belts that turned the blowers to the point where they were barely working. Then the blower stopped working and smoke and deadly gas from the fires began to fill the engine room.

Stimers, engineer Isaac Newton, and several other men rushed into the engine room. They managed to mend the broken belt, but before they could get the blower started, the second belt broke. Stimers later wrote, "The fires burned with a sickly blaze, converting all the air in the engine and firerooms into carbonic-acid-gas, a few inhalations of which are sufficient to destroy animal life."[22]

The men with him began to stagger from the poisonous smoke. Stimers, the senior officer, ordered everyone out. He stayed behind, trying to get a blower going, but was not successful. He later wrote that "I soon began to find myself getting very limber in the legs, so I started also for the top of the turret, which I managed to reach just as my strength gave out and I tumbled over upon the turret deck at full length."[23]

The water continued to pour into the ship. The steam pumps, normally able to handle leaks, were not working. The lack of air for ventilation was also causing the boiler fires to go out, and these boilers ran the pumps. The engine room was uninhabitable. Unfortunately, since one of the fleeing engineers had left the door open, the smoke and gas were spreading throughout the ship. Keeler had rushed down to the engine room and was about to shut the door, when a sailor told him that he thought a man was left inside. Despite the danger, Keeler and the sailor rescued the man and brought him up to the top of the turret.

Executive Officer Lieutenant Greene was also working to get the men out from the lower decks when he began to be overcome by the gas. Greene barely got out in time. All the men were topside, virtually all crowded on top of the turret. They were safe — for the moment. The engines had stopped, so gas was no longer spewing out, but water was still coming into the ship. The steam pumps, designed for such a situation, were not working and the hand pumps could not bring water out from the lower deck through the turret. A bucket brigade was formed but it did little more than keep the men occupied, so they might spend less time thinking that the ship was still in trouble. The *Monitor* was dead weight at the end of a 400-yard (366-meter) tow-rope from the *Seth Low*.

Captain Worden was still ill, so Lieutenant Greene's next step was to run up the American flag upside down. This was, and still is, a sign of distress. Unfortunately, the *Monitor*'s two escort vessels, the *Sachem* and the *Currituck*, were themselves having a lot of trouble with the storm and could not help. Greene, however, was finally able to establish contact with the *Seth Low* and ordered its captain to pull the *Monitor* toward shore, where the water was calmer.

John L. Worden, captain of the U.S.S. *Monitor* during its fight with the *Virginia*. After recovering from the wound he received during the battle, Worden went on to a distinguished career in the navy during and after the Civil War. He eventually reached the rank of rear admiral.

This trip, only a few miles, took five hours.

By 8:00 P.M. on the night of March 7, the situation looked a lot better. The seas were far calmer closer to shore and the gas had cleared from the ship. Stimers had first fixed the blower belts and restarted the ventilation system. Soon after, the fires were restarted, along with the engines and the steam pump, which emptied the water from the lower deck. When the ship got under way, with Stimers the first engineer to recover, Keeler stood watch over the engine.

Greene stood the four-hour watch until midnight. The situation seemed sufficiently back to normal, with a calm sea and moonlit clear sky. He told Captain Worden to remain in bed, and he, Greene, would take a nap with his clothes on to be available quickly if there was any trouble. Just a few minutes later, the *Monitor* passed a shoal. Greene then heard a loud and unpleasant noise; another storm had come up suddenly, with the wind blowing directly at the *Monitor.* A particularly large wave shot through the anchor well and into what was called the "hawse pipe," the opening through which the anchor chain came out from the chain locker inside the ship. Even worse, waves began to break over the blower vent openings, raising the risk of another near disaster, or total disaster, with the ventilation system.

The wheel ropes connecting the helm (the control center) with the rudder then jumped off the wheel. The ship began to wobble back and forth, risking breaking the tow-rope from the *Seth Low*. Fortunately, it held. By 3:00 A.M., the *Monitor* reached calmer waters. The rest of March 8 passed with no problems.

Later that afternoon, the *Monitor* passed Cape Henry, the entrance to Chesapeake Bay. Keller later wrote,

> We imagined we heard heavy firing in the distance.
> . . . As we neared the land, clouds of smoke could be
> seen hanging over it in the direction of [Fort Monroe,
> their destination], & as we approached still nearer
> little black spots could occasionally be seen suddenly
> springing into the air, remaining stationary for a
> moment or two & then gradually expanding into a
> large white cloud.[24]

THE C.S.S. *VIRGINIA* GETS READY

The launching of the *Virginia* was rather anticlimactic for a ship destined to make naval history. There was no ceremony. No special guests attended, not even the senior officers. When water began to fill the dry dock and the ship slid out into the river, the most senior of the five marines aboard was a corporal. It was christened the C.S.S. *Virginia,* but most people on both sides still used the name *Merrimack*. It leaked and still needed work. Some of this work, including putting protective iron shutters on the gun ports, would not be finished when the ship saw action. The crack in one of the supports for the ram attached to the bow was never fixed.

While the final touches were being put on the *Virginia*, Stephen Mallory had to find someone to command the ship. He came up with an unusual arrangement in choosing the ship's captain—he did not choose one. Lieutenant Catesby ap Roger Jones, in charge of the ship during the second half of its construction, wanted the command. But, under the strict seniority system in both navies, Jones was too young at age 41 and too junior in rank. (Things were different in the armies. Both sides would have generals in their twenties.) Several officers senior to Jones had applied for the command and Mallory thought it would create problems if Jones got the job.

These applicants were also senior to Mallory's choice, 61-year-old Captain Franklin Buchanan. Buchanan joined the U.S. navy in 1815 at age 14, eventually rising to the rank of captain. In 1861, thinking that Maryland would succeed, he resigned his commission but turned over his last command, the Washington Navy Yard, to his successor. When Maryland did not leave the Union, Buchanan asked to be reinstated but Welles personally denied his request. Buchanan went home to his estate in Maryland to sulk. Within a few months, however, he responded to hints from the Confederate government that he would receive a high rank if he joined the Confederate navy. Mallory made him a captain.

Mallory's concession to naval politics was to appoint Buchanan to command the James River defenses, with the *Virginia* as his flagship. Since neither side had admirals yet, Buchanan became what is known as a "flag officer," meaning that he was authorized to fly his personal flag aboard his "flagship." Buchanan received his orders on February 24, 1862. He had less than three weeks to get his ship ready for action.

Franklin Buchanan, shown well before the Civil War as a lieutenant in the U.S. navy. Buchanan had joined the navy in 1815, at age 14, and served until 1861, rising to the rank of captain. Buchanan's actual title at the time the C.S.S. *Virginia* went into action was "commander of the James River defenses." For political reasons, the *Virginia* never actually had a captain, but served as the flagship for Buchanan and his successor. Buchanan later became the senior Confederate admiral.

March 8

Military secrecy tends to deal with "when" and "where," rather than "what." With the *Virginia*, it was really just a case of when. The Union commanders knew the ship was going to go after their blockading fleet at anchor in Hampton Roads. The question was when.

On March 1, 1862, the Union tugboat *Dragon* met a small Confederate boat under a flag of truce in Hampton Roads. Passengers traveling north were transferred to the *Dragon*. While this was going on, the Union engineer asked his Confederate counterpart "How about this old *Merrimack*?" The Confederate replied, "Oh, she's all right. . . . She may be out in about a week."[25]

By March 8, the *Virginia* finally had enough ammunition.

The weather, however, was not cooperating—though not to the extent it endangered the *Monitor* that day. Buchanan had planned to steam out at night, March 6, up the Elizabeth River to just off Newport News. Early the next morning he planned to attack and sink the two main Union vessels, the *Congress* and the *Cumberland*. However, Buchanan was told that the five pilots who would guide the ship into Hampton Roads refused to do so at night. They refused to risk a large, heavy, slow-moving, untested vessel on tricky waters.

Early in the morning of March 8, a Union signal officer at Fort Monroe noticed that a French naval vessel in Hampton Roads was getting up steam, as if it were planning to move. The French had not given notice of any intent to head out to sea, in keeping with custom, so the fort could fire a salute. The Union forces realized that the French, whose neutrality would require them not to report anything they might have learned, might have been tipped off to an impending attack. They might be preparing to get out of the way of artillery fire between the fort and an attacking vessel.

Only Captain Buchanan knew the second interesting event of that morning. He received a confidential letter from Secretary of War Mallory. Mallory had previously suggested that, if successful in Hampton Roads, the *Virginia* should sail up the Potomac and shell Washington, D.C. This letter proposed instead that the *Virginia*'s second action should be to pass out of the Chesapeake Bay, sail up the coast, and shell New York City. Buchanan would not be able to answer Mallory for several days.

The casemate of the *Virginia* was spread with tallow, a type of grease. This was supposed to increase the chance that cannonballs would harmlessly deflect off the ship. Workmen were still working up to the time of departure; a few even had to jump onto the dock as the ship pulled away.

Crowds lined both banks of the Elizabeth as the *Virginia* steamed north. Some members of the crew later recalled thinking that the crowd might not be there just to see the *Virginia*, but to see it sink. What they did see was a very odd-looking craft, a gigantic floating barn roof, as it was described, that was neither fast nor maneuverable. Buchanan realized how slow the ship was moving and called the men for lunch. H. Ashton Ramsay, the *Virginia*'s chief engineer, recalled being about to sit down to eat in the wardroom when he noticed, at one end, the ship's surgeon laying out his instruments. Ramsay lost his appetite.

When the *Virginia* left the dock, only a few people, including Secretary Malloy, Jones, and the captains of the three smaller vessels in his James River squadron, knew Buchanan's plans. However, Ramsay must have gotten a strong hint when, just before departure, Buchanan came to talk to him for a few moments. Buchanan asked, "What would happen to your engines and boilers, if there should be a collision?" Ramsay replied that though they were large, they were braced tightly to the engine deck. Collisions would not hurt them. "I am going to ram the *Cumberland*. I'm told she has the new rifled guns, the only ones in their whole fleet we have cause to fear. The moment we are out in the Roads I am going to make right for her and ram her."[26]

Buchanan then asked Ramsay if the engines needed a trial run. Ramsay responded that the ten-mile (16-kilometer) trip to the Union fleet would be sufficient test.

Two smaller steamers, the *Raleigh* and the *Beaufort*, accompanied the *Virginia*. Unlike the *Virginia*'s crew, their captains knew Buchanan's plans. They also knew that Buchanan had warned them of a new signal they might receive—to fight until they were sunk, not to surrender under any conditions. At 12:30, the *Beaufort* took the *Virginia* under tow to help with steering. The *Virginia*'s keel was now very close to the bottom of the river, which made the rudder even less responsive than usual. Not long after this, the *Virginia* passed a point of land two miles (three kilometers) north of Norfolk. The Confederates now had a clear view

An Outsider's View, Selections from the Report of the Commander of the French Naval Vessel *Gassendi*

About 12:40 [March 8, 1862]. A mass, having the appearance of a barrack's roof surmounted by a large funnel, appeared at the entrance of Elizabeth River, a little inside of Sewell's Point. Everyone recognized the *Merrimac* immediately.

. . . Not one of [the Union] vessels appeared to notice the arrival of their formidable enemy in the Roads, and it was more than a quarter of an hour after her appearance that a shot fired by one of the gunboats announced that she was in sight.

. . . The *Merrimac*, however, [ignored Union fire and headed] toward the frigates which she wished to destroy. . . . She was immediately greeted by a violent cannonade from the two frigates and from the batteries of Newport News. The Confederate battery at Pig Point replied. The fight was then hidden from us in a great measure by the point, which allowed us to see only the masts of the frigates; but we were able to estimate the force of the fire, which during a quarter of an hour, particularly, was of the hottest.

. . . This vessel, after having delivered a broadside at the *Congress*, the nearest of the two frigates, advanced toward the *Cumberland*, whose formidable battery might well be dreaded, and struck her amidships at a speed of four or five knots, partially breaking her ram.

. . . Everything [for the Union side] seemed desperate on the evening of the eighth, and a general panic appeared to take possession of everyone. The terrible engine of war, so often announced, had at length appeared, and in an hour at most had destroyed two of the strongest ships of the Union, silenced two powerful land batteries and seen the rest of the naval force which the day before blockaded the two rivers, retreat before her. . . . Everything was in confusion at Fortress Monroe; ferryboats, gunboats, and tugboats were coming and going in all directions; drums and bugles beat and sounded with unusual spirit.

of Hampton Roads through the mouth of the Elizabeth River. Somewhat to the left of Fort Monroe, they could see Buchanan's designated targets, the U.S.S. *Congress* and the U.S.S. *Cumberland*.

. . . [The next day, March 9, the C.S.S. *Virginia* and the U.S.S. *Monitor*] engaged in the fight at first at long range, but the two enemies were not slow in coming together, each one striving to find the weak spot in the armor of her adversary. In this contest of naval tactics, entirely in a narrow channel of little depth, the *Monitor*, whose draft is not half that of the *Merrimac*, had an enormous advantage over the latter. Sure of her workings she could run at full speed, approach or retired, as she judged best, without fear of running aground. The Confederate battery, on the contrary, could not move nor perform any evolutions except with the greatest precaution, in spite of the evident great skill of her pilot.

At the commencement of the action [the *Virginia*] grounded and remained immovable for a quarter of an hour. However, the fight continued with an equal ardor. Several times in their evolutions the two adversaries fired upon each other at a distance of a few meters, and in spite of their powerful batteries the projectiles bounded off perfectly harmless, apparently. Once the *Merrimac* ran into the *Monitor*, but whether her ram had been completely broken the day before or whether it was placed too high, she struck her enemy at the water line and produced only a slight depression on the powerful armor plating which protected that part. Shortly after, the flagstaff of the *Merrimac* was shot away by a ball, and the tops in the Roads, as well as the ramparts of the fortress, saluted this accident with frantic hurrahs as a victory. But soon a sailor appeared on the gratings, showing at the end of a staff the flag which had for an instant disappeared.

Source: United States Department of the Navy, *Official Records of the Union and Confederate Navies in the War of the Rebellion*, Washington, D.C.: Government Printing Office, 1897, Series I, Volume 6, pages 69–72.

As far as the Confederates could see, and they were still some miles off, they were not expected. Both Union ships had their launch boats hanging out on booms, ready to lower to send people ashore and to receive visitors. The seamen had hung their washing in the rigging to dry. For the Union sailors, at least for the moment, it was a relaxed Saturday morning, a rare nice day in a cold winter. The Confederates were more anxious, anticipating the coming battle. With the slow approach toward their enemy, however, some of the Confederate officers had time to remember back before the Civil War, when they had served on the *Congress* or the *Cumberland*.

The Confederates had achieved some tactical surprise with their timing. Perhaps this was due to the series of previous reports and rumors that the "*Merrimac* was coming out," which had turned out to be false.

The *Virginia* continued toward its targets. By this time, about 1:00 P.M., at least the Union crews noticed the ship. Union sailors were seen staring in the direction of the oncoming steam-belching monster, a floating barn with cannons, as some later described the *Virginia*. Confederates did notice that smaller craft were leaving the center of the Roads to take shelter near Fort Monroe. They appeared to be getting out of the way of the upcoming action.

Soon, both targeted Union warships hoisted signal flags, probably to warn Fort Monroe and other ships of the approaching enemy. The launch boats were either pulled up or sent to shore. Smoke was seen coming from two other major Union warships in the distance on the other side of Fort Monroe, the U.S.S. *Minnesota* and the U.S.S. *Roanoke*. Captain John Marston, senior Union naval officer at Hampton Roads, had ordered the *Minnesota* to immediately go to the assistance of the two ships targeted by Buchanan. The *Minnesota* was quickly under way, but would take about an hour to get there. The *Roanoke*, whose engines were still awaiting repair, would have to be towed into action. Even so, both were soon under way. The *Congress* and the *Cumberland* went to battle stations.

Only now did Buchanan tell his men what they probably already knew: that this was not a test run. "Sailors, in a few minutes you will have the long-looked-for opportunity of showing your devotion to our cause. Remember that you are about to strike for your country and your homes. The Confederacy expects every man to do his duty. Beat to quarters."[27]

About 1:30, the *Virginia* passed through the mouth of the Elizabeth River and entered Hampton Roads. Union batteries at Fort Monroe and on the northern shore of Hampton Roads were already firing, but falling short of their targets. The gunners knew the *Virginia* was a large, impressive, and dangerous ship, but did not yet know how little difference hitting the target would make. About 2:00 P.M., acting without orders, the captain of the U.S.S. *Beaufort* fired an ineffective shot against the *Congress*.

A few moments later, about a mile from the *Cumberland*, Buchanan ordered his bow gun to fire the first "official" Confederate shot of the battle at that ship. The shot passed through the starboard side, the right side of the ship, sending splinters flying, which wounded several sailors. The *Cumberland* soon responded but the shot missed. As the gun crew was reloading, the *Virginia* bow gun fired again. The shell exploded in the middle of the same gun crew that was busy reloading. Every man was killed except for the powder boy and the gun captain in charge of the gun. The gun captain had both arms shot off at the shoulder.

The *Congress*, commanded by Lieutenant Joseph B.

The U.S.S. *Cumberland*, shown in 1843, in a lithograph by Nathaniel Currier. Currier later joined with J. Merritt Ives to form the famous team called "Currier & Ives."

Smith, son of the Commodore Smith of the Welles's ironclad board, was anchored several hundred yards south of the *Cumberland*. The crew of the *Congress* was already firing at the *Virginia* as it approached both ships. At about 2:30 P.M., the ships were only about 300 yards (274 meters) apart, easy shooting range for naval cannons of the time. The *Congress* fired a broadside at the *Virginia*, discharging all of the guns on one side of the ship. Since most of the shells and cannonballs hit their target, this would have heavily damaged most opposing wooden warships. The crew of the *Virginia*, however, barely noticed the volley. One officer, though, did think it fortunate that none of the Union shots came in through the open gun ports. Buchanan had not wanted to wait for the protective iron shutters to be installed.

The *Virginia* had only four cannons on each side, but they fired far more powerful shells than the cannons on the Union ships. Two of the Confederate cannons would be firing "hot shot." One shell went in a gun port, struck the gun carriage, threw the gun onto the deck, and killed or wounded the entire gun crew.

One of the hot shots passed through the ship, starting a fire on the port side that the crew could not put out. The other hot shot started a fire near the ship's ready ammunition magazine, in obvious danger of exploding the ammunition. The *Congress* kept shooting but had already taken very heavy damage. The *Virginia* steamed on toward the *Cumberland*.

A *New York Times* report describes its progress:

> Now she nears the *Cumberland* sloop of war, silent and still, wierd [*sic*] and mysterious, like some devilish and superhuman monster, or the horrid creation of a nightmare. Now, but a biscuit toss from the ship, and from the sides of both pour out a living tide of fire and smoke, or solid shot and heavy shell. We see from the ship's suppers running streams of crimson gore.[28]

The *Virginia* drew closer to the *Cumberland*. The Union crew kept firing, though they could see that their shots were having no effect. They could also see the ram at the front of their enemy. Ramsay, on the *Virginia*, had another conversation with his boss. Buchanan ordered Ramsay to reverse engines as soon as the *Virginia* hit the *Cumberland*, without waiting for orders. Back in the engine room, Ramsay soon heard the signal to stop engines and then the signal to reverse engines. Ramsay followed the orders. There is no indication whether Buchanan gave the orders too soon, or whether he wanted to make it easier for his ship to withdraw after hitting the *Cumberland*.

Only some of the crew of the *Virginia* heard anything as their ship first crashed through timbers protecting the *Cumberland* from floating mines and then into the Union ship itself. Some barely felt the crash. In other areas of the ship, the impact of the crash on the *Virginia* was very noticeable. The shock was more noticeable on the *Cumberland* but less violent than might have been expected. It did open a hole in the *Cumberland*, about seven feet (two meters) wide, totally underwater. The bottom deck of the *Cumberland* was almost instantly flooded; the ship was doomed.

The Union ship almost immediately began to list to starboard, tilting to its right side. The *Cumberland* caught the *Virginia*'s ram and began forcing the *Virginia* down by the bow. The *Virginia* could be taken down with the *Cumberland* when the latter ship sank. The crew of the *Cumberland* had a brief opportunity to sink the *Virginia* but failed to realize it. The Confederates were directly beneath the Union ship's starboard anchor. Had they dropped the anchor, it had a good chance of securing the *Virginia*. Soon the *Virginia*, propelled by a fortunate wave, drifted to a different angle. The *Cumberland* rolled slightly away from the *Virginia* and the latter was able to back out. The ram, however, broke off.

The steady fire from the *Cumberland*'s guns did not let up. This says a lot for the devotion to duty of the Union sailors, particularly since most would have realized that the ship was going to sink. The uselessness of the fire also says a lot for the advantages of iron armor. Many of the shots were hitting the *Virginia*, making a lot of noise inside the ship, but bouncing off harmlessly. Barring a lucky shot that entered a gun port, this noisemaking would continue. An iron ship that could just sail straight into battle, with no concern about enemy fire, was effectively invincible.

This battle no doubt had one of the largest nonpartic-ipant audiences in naval history. Both sides of Hampton Roads were lined with spectators, their sympathies depending on which side of the water they stood. Some Confederate spectators on Sewell's Point to the southeast of the battle complained they could not see very well without "spyglasses," a term used to mean either small, handheld telescopes or binoculars. Another witness, Confederate Colonel Raleigh Colston, was on Ragged Island, directly across the water only three to four miles from the fight. He could see clearly, but could not hear. "We could see every flash of the guns and the clouds of white smoke, but not a single report was audible."[29] Seeing was enough, apparently: "I could hardly believe my eyes when I saw the masts of the *Cumberland* begin to sway wildly."[30]

The audience on the north side of Hampton Roads was far less happy about what they were seeing. A reporter described the *Virginia* ramming the *Cumberland* "Like a rhinoceros . . . with a dead, soul-rendering crunch she pierces her on the starboard bow, lifting her up as a man does a toy."[31]

For at least another half hour, the *Cumberland* and the *Virginia* kept firing at each other. A few Union shots actually caused damage. Union gunners realized that they might be able to get shells inside the *Virginia*'s portholes. After firing a shot, the Confederate's bow gun sponger, who washed the barrel down between shots, got a bit too enthusiastic. He started working while standing in the porthole of the bow gun, and was cut in half by a Union shell. As the ironclad was backing off its target, a Union shell hit the forward port broadside gun and exploded, breaking off a foot of muzzle, killing a man and wounding the rest of the gun crew. Another shot hit a loaded hotshot gun, breaking two feet off of its muzzle. However, the impact caused the gun to fire and, at that short range, hit the *Cumberland*.

This just added additional damage to the *Cumberland*, smashed above the waterline in addition to the large hole in its hull. One shell hit the sickbay, killing four already wounded crewmen. Other wounded would drown as the ship sank, unable to move. The deck of the ship was described as slippery with blood from the killed and the wounded. The only positive development on the ship was that there was no explosion as it sank, perhaps because rising water flooded the remaining gunpowder. Just after 3:00 P.M., the executive officer of the *Cumberland*, in command in the absence of the captain, ordered, "Every man look out for himself!"[32]

In the relatively shallow water, when the *Cumberland* settled to the bottom, its masts remained above water. Observers noted that the flag was still flying. Casualty figures for the fight were approximate, but the closest estimate is that about 376 were on board that day, of which about 121 were killed, with many more wounded.

THE *VIRGINIA* TAKES ON A SECOND TARGET

Smoke from the *Virginia*'s own guns made it impossible for anyone on board to see what was happening on the *Cumberland*. But Buchanan sensed, quite accurately, that the ship was sinking. He decided to go after his second target, the already damaged *Congress*. This was not as easy as it seemed. Buchanan would have to sail the *Virginia* into the James River, and then slowly turn around. The ship's keel dragged in the mud of the shallow channel, making steering even harder. It would take almost an hour for the *Virginia* to turn and get back to the *Congress*.

The crew of the *Congress* began to cheer at what they

Twenty years after the view of the U.S.S. *Cumberland* shown earlier, Currier joined with Ives to produce a grimmer view of the ship, showing its destruction on March 8, 1862, at the hands of the C.S.S. *Virginia.*

thought was the sight of the *Virginia* steaming away from battle. The stern pivot gun of the *Virginia* then fired three very effective shots into the *Congress.* The result was to destroy or damage two of the stern guns on the *Congress.*

The *Virginia* had company when it completed the turn. The small James River flotilla, under Commander John R. Tucker, had run past the Union batteries at Newport News. The *Patrick Henry* was hit, and had to be towed out of action. The other two ships, however, could assist the *Virginia*, which did not seem to need much assistance. At the same time, about 3:30 P.M., the U.S.S. *Minnesota,* coming to the aid of the *Congress*, ran aground in shallow water—over a shoal dividing Hampton Roads into two channels—about a mile and half away. The *Roanoke* had run aground earlier. To preserve the pattern, somewhat later the U.S.S. *St. Lawrence* and its 52 guns, the most powerful ship in the area except, of course, for the *Virginia*, also ran aground. These ships were firing on the *Virginia*, but at too long a range to even hope to have an effect. At the same time, Confederate batteries on Sewell's Point, north of Norfolk, were shooting at them.

Lieutenant Joseph Smith, captain of the *Congress* and the son of Commodore Joseph Smith from Welles's ironclad board, decided to try to ground his ship. He thought this would protect it from ramming, at least. Smith signaled to the small Union steamer *Zouave* to leave the clearly sinking *Cumberland* and come to his ship. The *Zouave* fastened a line to the *Congress*, still on fire, and began to tow it toward shore.

Just before about 4:00 P.M., the *Virginia* came within 200 yards (183 meters) of the *Congress* and opened fire. Some shots hit the *Zouave* but most smashed into the stern of the *Congress*. At about 4:20, Smith was killed by a shell that took off his head. By 4:30, little remained of the stern of the *Congress*, unable to return the continuing fire from the *Virginia*. Lieutenant Austin Pendergrast, who had taken over as captain, began moving the many wounded from sickbay to the main deck. They would be put in boats and sent ashore. By now, however, the Confederate ships *Beaufort*, *Yorktown*, and *Patrick Henry* (which had been repaired) arrived and joined in the fight.

After an hour of this pounding, Pendergrast realized he had no option but to surrender his ship. He ordered the flag lowered, and then a white flag raised. (The *Zouave* did not surrender and was able to escape, but with damage to its rudder.) When Buchanan saw the white flag, he ordered his guns to stop firing. He then signaled the *Beaufort* to come within hailing distance so he could talk with Commander Parker, its captain. Parker was told to formally receive the surrender of the ship, take its officers prisoner, let the men go ashore, and then set the ship on fire.

Something went wrong during this process. The smaller Confederate vessels had come within range of rifle fire from the Union troops on shore. Earlier that afternoon, one of the *Virginia*'s occasional shell shots toward shore had hit the headquarters of Brigadier General Joseph Mansfield but did not explode. Had the shell exploded, Mansfield would likely have been killed. The *Virginia* spent the rest of the battle out of range. However, this changed for the smaller Confederate vessels. Mansfield ordered two companies from the Union 20th Indiana infantry to open fire on the smaller ships. When reminded by one of his officers that the *Congress* had surrendered, Mansfield sharply replied that he had not.

Union fire chased off Parker and his two ships, but it also hit some of the men on the *Congress*, killing several. Parker realized he had to withdraw, and his ships immediately steamed away from the area. Buchanan, however, did not realize that the *Congress* and any ships next to it were in range of Union rifle fire from the shore. Parker did not report to Buchanan, who thought the failure to burn the ship was Parker's fault. Buchanan ordered another party to go burn the ship and sent the *Teaser* as escort. This second party, in the small boat from the *Virginia*, was also chased off. This time, however, the *Teaser* reported what had happened.

Buchanan was livid. He ordered the *Virginia* to steam close to the *Congress* and destroy it. The *Congress* was pounded, with more fires started in several places. Still in a rage, Buchanan took a rifle, went to an exposed position on the top deck, and began shooting back at the Union soldiers on the shore. They returned fire and Buchanan was soon seriously wounded in the left thigh. Lieutenant Catesby ap Jones was ordered to take command and continue the fight as long as possible.

The End of the U.S.S. *Congress*

Fifty years after the battle, the chief engineer of the C.S.S. *Virginia*, H. Ashton Ramsay, remembered watching the U.S.S. *Congress* burn on the night of March 8, 1862.

> All the evening we stood on deck watching the brilliant display of the burning ship. Every part of her was on fire at the same time, the red-tongues flames running up shrouds, masts, and stays, and extending out to the yard arms. She stood in bold relief against the black background, lighting up the Roads and reflecting her lurid lights on the bosom of the now placid and hushed waters. Every now and then the flames would reach one of the loaded cannon and a shell would hiss at random through the darkness. About midnight came the grand finale. The magazines exploded, shooting up a huge column of firebrands hundreds of feet in the air, and then the burning hulk burst asunder and melted into the waters, while the calm night spread her sable mantle over Hampton Roads.

Source: H. Ashton Ramsay, "The Most Famous of Sea Duels," *Harper's Weekly*, February 10, 1912, Volume 61, page 13.

The sun was setting. The *Jamestown* and the *Patrick Henry* were already exchanging fire with the U.S.S. *Minnesota* and doing damage. The *Virginia* fired a few shots. However, the target was in a position that made it hard for the *Virginia* to get close. The pilots told Jones that this particular part of the Roads was hard to navigate during the day and downright dangerous at night. Jones fired a parting shot and then anchored near the Confederate positions at Sewell's Point. The first day's battle, the worst day the U.S. navy would have until Pearl Harbor, 90 years later, was over. There were, however, two postscripts.

Just after midnight, the flames from fires on the *Congress* reached the gunpowder. It blew up spectacularly, heard

U.S.S. Congress, *depicted during better days in the harbor of Naples, Italy, in 1857. The U.S.S.* Susquehanna *is the other large vessel shown.*

and seen all over the Hampton Roads area. Union sailors, hearing the explosion, swore revenge. The next postscript came early the next morning. When the *Virginia* was steaming out on March 9, 1862, to finish off the *Minnesota*, some crewmen noticed what seemed to be a raft with a boiler on top next to their designated target. Others thought it looked like a cheese box on a raft. A few guessed what this odd-looking craft, which had been anchored next to the *Minnesota* since just past midnight, actually was.

A few minutes after 8:00 A.M., the U.S.S. *Monitor* steamed out to engage the C.S.S. *Virginia* and opened fire.

March 9

6

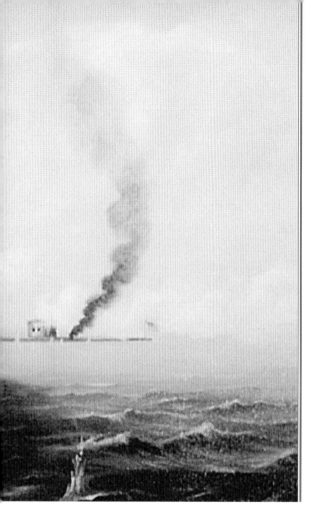

A modern painting by Raymond Bayless shows the battle between the U.S.S. *Monitor* and the C.S.S. *Virginia*. The U.S.S. *Minnesota* is to the left of the *Virginia*.

INTERLUDE IN HAMPTON ROADS

One can guess that few senior officers slept much on the night of March 8 in the Hampton Roads area. The Confederates had the better night, though. They had just come off a good day, one in which they destroyed two major Union warships. They expected a better day to follow, when the *Virginia* had an opportunity to destroy three more, starting with the U.S.S. *Minnesota* stuck in the middle of Hampton Roads. The captain of the *Minnesota* anticipated similar results. He informed Captain John Marston, commanding Union naval forces in Hampton Roads, that the *Minnesota* could not be floated. Part of the crew would be sent ashore. The result, likely volunteers, would stay to

83

fight to the end and the *Minnesota* would be blown up to prevent its capture.

Around 9:00 P.M., about the time Captain Marston was sitting onboard his flagship, the *Roanoke*, and reading the day's communications, the U.S.S. *Monitor* arrived and anchored nearby. Worden and Stimers immediately went over to talk with Marston. They learned what happened that day, part of which they had heard from a distance. They learned that the *Virginia* was expected out the next day, to finish the job of destroying the Union fleet. Worden also learned that Marston was holding orders from Welles to send the *Monitor* to Washington, D.C.

Marston immediately proposed, and Worden agreed, to disobey Welles's orders and keep the *Monitor* at Hampton Roads. Worden was then ordered to anchor next to the *Minnesota* and await the *Virginia*. Worden took a few minutes to telegraph his arrival to Welles. Several hours were then spent finding a pilot willing and able to guide the *Monitor* through the complicated shoals of Hampton Roads to the *Minnesota*. By 1:00 A.M. however, the ironclad was in position. A few hours later, just as the crewmen on the *Monitor* were getting to sleep, the ship was hailed by the *Minnesota*. The *Minnesota* was finally afloat, but could the *Monitor* please get out of the way. The *Monitor* had to back away. It took an hour to discover that the *Minnesota* was still stuck.

INTERLUDE IN WASHINGTON

Major General John Wool, commanding Union troops in the Fort Monroe area, that evening sent a telegram to the secretary of war in Washington, notifying Edwin Stanton of the destruction of the Union navy. The morning of March 9, 1862, a Sunday, Welles was at the Navy Department when he received a copy of Wool's message. Minutes later, he was summoned to the White House for an emergency cabinet meeting. Arriving at the White House, aside from the rest of the cabinet and the president, Welles found John Dahlgren, commandant of the Washington Navy Yard, and Montgomery Meigs, army quartermaster general.

Stanton was tense and excited, seemingly almost in a panic, pacing up and down the cabinet room, glaring at the calm Welles. Welles later wrote that

> the most frightened man on that gloomy day, the most so I think of any during the Rebellion, was the Secretary of War. He was at times almost frantic, and as he walked the room with his eyes fixed on me, I saw well the [presumably negative] estimation in which he held me with my unmoved and unexcited manner and conversation . . . there was throughout the whole day something inexpressibly ludicrous in the wild, frantic talk, action, and rage of Stanton as he ran from room to room, sat down and jumped up after writing a few words, swung his arms, scolded, and raved.[33]

Welles noted that even the president, a man not known to panic, would occasionally get up and look out the window to the Potomac River.

Stanton was new to the cabinet, having joined only about a month before. He remained temperamental, frequently hard to deal with, but people eventually realized that he was also tough and effective. March 9 was clearly not a high point in his career. Stanton was not calmed by Welles's statement that he expected the *Monitor* to handle the *Virginia*. Even if victorious, the *Virginia* was too sluggish to take into the Atlantic and too heavy with too deep a draft to come up the Potomac and attack Washington. There was no need or advantage to Stanton's plan to block the Potomac by sinking stone-laden barges, presented at a second cabinet meeting that day. Such a move, in fact, would only seal off Washington to Union vessels. Fortunately, when Stanton actually had Dahlgren prepare the barges, Lincoln ordered that the barges only be sunk if the *Virginia* actually approached Washington.

However, the *Virginia* was busy elsewhere.

HAMPTON ROADS

After figuring out what the *Monitor* was, the Confederates faced the problem of how to handle it. At the very least, March 9 would not be a day for the easy destruction of wooden enemy ships. An officer on the *Virginia* wrote about the *Monitor*, "She could not possibly have made her appearance at a more inopportune time."[34]

Union witnesses, interestingly enough, were not all that impressed with the new arrival. Edward Shippen, surgeon from the *Congress*, later wrote about first seeing the *Monitor*,

> suddenly there glided out from under the shadow of the [U.S.S. *Minnesota*] . . . a raft-like vessel almost flush with the water, and bearing on her deck a black turret. At first, no one in our camp seemed to know what it was or how it came there, but at last it was conceded that it must be the strange new ironclad which we had heard was being built in New York by Ericsson. . . . She seemed so small and trifling that we feared she would only constitute additional prey for the leviathan.[35]

The *Monitor* moved closer to the *Minnesota* after dawn. The crew of the *Monitor* could see the holes in its far larger neighbor, made by the *Virginia*'s shells the day before. They could also see crewmen from the *Minnesota* throwing their duffel bags onto tugs, as well as ship's stores. The *Minnesota*'s captain was making one last effort, with the *Virginia* approaching, to lighten his ship and get it afloat. If this failed, the captain was going to destroy his own ship.

When they saw the *Virginia*, the men of the *Monitor* went to battle stations. The deck hatches were shut, the smokestack and vent stacks were removed, and protective coverings were put on the glass skylights. William Keeler, as paymaster, had no battle station, so he remained on top of the turret with a few others. A moment after a shot from the *Virginia* sailed over them and hit the *Minnesota*, Captain Worden came up and suggested that they might want to get below.

The turret, lit only by some sunlight from gratings on the top of the tower and some lanterns, was dark and shadowy. No one was moving or speaking. With the shutters closed, no one in the turret could actually see the *Virginia*. Keeler would later describe his own feelings not really as fear, but as concern and suspense. The crew did not know if the *Monitor*, however carefully designed, would work. The men soon heard several single shots pass over, probably from the *Virginia*, and then many guns firing at once, likely a broadside from the *Minnesota*.

Executive Officer Greene, commanding the guns in the turret, sent Keeler forward to ask Captain Worden if he should fire. The speaking tube was not working. Worden told Greene to wait, as his ship headed straight at the *Virginia*. A few moments later, Worden's next message was: Commence firing. The engines stopped, the turret was turned to face the enemy, the shutters were opened, a gun run out, the lanyard pulled, and the shot was fired. (Interestingly, no one seems to have recorded whether the shot hit or missed.) A *Monitor* crewmember, who looked out after the first shot, later remarked about the *Virginia* that "You can see surprise on a ship just the same as you can see it in a human being, and there was surprise all over the *Merrimac*."[36]

Surprise the Confederates may have felt, but for the moment they made no change of plan. Flag Officer Buchanan was recovering from his wound the day before, so Lieutenant Jones was in charge. He realized what was shooting at his ship, but his intention was still to first finish off the *Minnesota*. Jones wanted to get within a half mile of the *Minnesota*, but was willing to settle for a range of a mile. When he did not even get that close, and in response to a continuing series of shots from the *Monitor*, he decided to fight the Union ironclad. The first naval battle between ironclad ships had begun.

They began shooting when they were about a mile and half from other, but closed to within 50 yards (46 meters)— closer that the average fight in the Civil War between Union and Confederate ground troops. The ships circled each other, at ranges from about 100 yards (91 meters) to virtually touching. The *Virginia* quickly found itself having problems aiming at the smaller, faster, more maneuverable target. The Confederates only saw the Union guns when they were about to fire. Greene saw the difficulty in raising the protective shutters over the gun ports. He solved this by keeping the shutters open and swinging the turret away from the *Virginia* to load the guns and back toward the Confederate to fire.

The *Monitor* also had a problem with aiming its guns. Greene had an opening of only a few inches between the guns and the turret. There was no way to get a better view, no real way to aim properly. The turret turning mechanism added to the problems by making it hard, almost impossible, to stop at a particular point. So Greene decided not to aim. Guns were fired on the fly, so to speak. Greene, who personally fired every shot, pulled the lanyard as the turret swung into position, and then quickly swung away. If Greene wanted to find out how well the shot did, he sent Keeler forward to the pilothouse, to ask Captain Worden. If

Thomas Catesby ap Roger Jones, executive officer of the C.S.S. *Virginia.* Due to Buchanan's wound on March 8, 1862, Jones commanded the *Virginia* during the battle with the *Monitor* the next day. This photo was probably taken a year or two after the battle and shows Jones after his promotion to commander.

Worden wanted to send instructions to Greene, he sent Keeler or Keeler's assistant aft to the turret. The Confederates wondered why the Union gunners were not stopping to aim. Greene was just making the best of a balky new ship.

This, however, prevented the Union crew from taking advantage of one of two ways the *Monitor* might have won a decisive victory over the *Virginia*. The *Monitor* was hitting its target with many of its shots. Most were just denting the *Virginia*'s armor, having as little effect as the hits the *Monitor* was taking. Some Union shots did crack armor plates, however. The Confederates thought that, had the *Monitor* concentrated on hitting the same spot, it might have punched a hole in the *Virginia*'s side and sent an explosive shell, with potentially disastrous results, inside the ship.

A second opportunity came as the *Virginia* began to ride higher and higher in the water as it used up coal. A well-aimed shot might have gone under the armor overhang and hit the *Virginia*'s unprotected lower hull. The Confederates could not guess that the *Monitor* could only fire one gun at a time, and that, due to instructions, was only using half the technically possible powder charge on each shot. Fully charged shots would have had a greater chance of cracking the *Virginia*'s armor. The Confederates had to do the best they could with a vessel that was leaking badly and was harder and harder to steer.

For two hours, the ironclads circled, blasting away at each other. Each shot that struck home, failing to do any perceptible damage, further proved how obsolete wooden vessels had become. If ironclads could not sink ironclads, if they could absorb each other's blows, what chance did a wooden ship have?

After two hours of inconclusive fighting, the Confederates came close to disaster. All of the circling in combat confused the pilots, and the *Virginia* ran aground. The *Monitor*, with half the draft of the *Virginia*, was able to circle the larger ship and keep firing. Union shots came close to breaking through the Confederate armor, or entering gun ports. Had they been able to keep it up for a few more minutes, they might have destroyed the *Virginia*.

Ashton Ramsay, chief engineer on the *Virginia*, was desperately trying to get his ship back into a deeper channel. He first disabled the safety valves on the boiler, which would keep the boiler from building up too much pressure. Anything that could burn, and particularly anything that would burn faster than coal, was thrown into the boilers. They were pushed well past the safety limits, but still did little more than help the propellers churn up mud. Boiler safety was no longer a concern.

The men on board thought it was a question of whether their own boilers or the *Monitor* would blow up their ship. The *Virginia* then lurched free and backed into the deeper channel. The men cheered. All but one of the *Virginia*'s guns resumed firing as they came into position. Acting Captain Jones, when he walked past the inactive gun station, asked the commander, "Why are you not firing, sir?" The officer responded, "It is quite a waste of ammunition to fire at her. Our powder is precious, and I find I can do the *Monitor* as much damage by snapping my finger at her every five minutes." Jones then responded, "Never mind, we are getting ready to ram her."[37]

Jones had not inspected the *Virginia* carefully enough the night before and apparently did not know that the ram had broken off. He then spoke with Ramsay, ordering Ramsay to reverse engines as soon as the ship hit the *Monitor*. The *Virginia* would only have half a mile to build up momentum, not the mile it normally required once it was aimed at the target. Jones also got cautious at the last minute, not wanting a repeat of the day before when the *Virginia* briefly got stuck after ramming the U.S.S. *Cumberland*. He ordered Ramsay to reverse engines before the two ships made contact.

Sitting up front in the *Monitor* pilothouse, Worden saw the *Virginia* coming and knew what Jones was attempting. He told Keeler to tell Greene to fire both guns. Worden also began turning his ship to get out of the way. Heading back to the turret, Keeler later wrote, "This was the critical moment, one that I had feared from the beginning of the fight—if she could so easily pierce the heavy oak beams of the *Cumberland*, she surely could go through the half-inch iron plates of our lower hull."[38] A few moments later, the crew of the *Monitor* felt the impact. The men looked for the hole, but found they were safe.

Virtually no damage was done to the *Monitor*. However, the *Virginia* developed a new leak in the bow. The pumps, as Ramsay had assured Jones, could handle the leak. The *Virginia* took further damage in its stern, near the pivot gun. Two Union shells, fired almost simultaneously when the ships made contact, hit the *Virginia*. The side was dented several inches and the men in the area were all knocked down by the concussion. Fortunately for the crew of the *Virginia*, the Union gunners did not hit that same spot again.

Several members of the crew of the *Monitor* had a similar experience. They were in the turret, leaning against the wall, when a Confederate shot hit right outside the spot where they were standing. One, Stimers, was virtually uninjured. The second man, leaning his knee against the turret, was knocked unconscious and thrown to the deck. The third had his head near the wall where the Confederate shell struck. He was knocked out by the inside air pressure from the blast.

Not long after this, the *Monitor* ran out of ammunition in the turret. It still had a good supply of ammunition below deck, but to bring it into the turret, the turret would have to stop moving so its hatch could align with the one in the main deck. Worden did not want to risk a well-placed enemy shot hitting the turret while shells and powder were being carried up. He pulled out of the fight for a half hour. It was 11:00 A.M.

Period depiction of the March 9, 1862, fight between the U.S.S. *Monitor* and the C.S.S. *Virginia.* The *Virginia* should be shown somewhat larger, relative to the *Monitor.*

Jones took advantage of the respite from the *Monitor* to start firing regularly at the *Minnesota.* One shot started a fire, which the Union crew quickly extinguished. A second hit and exploded the boiler of a Union tug near the *Minnesota.*

Soon after the *Monitor* resumed action, the two ironclads were again approaching each other, possibly even touching, firing at very close range. Jones was realizing that he could do little damage to the *Monitor.* Some officers proposed boarding the ship. Volunteers from the *Virginia* would jump onto the flat deck of the *Monitor,* carrying hammers and wedges to drive between the deck and the turret and keep the turret from moving. A Southern seaman was actually on his way to put his sea jacket over the viewing slit of the pilothouse when he was stopped by an officer.

The *Monitor*'s crew was not concerned about boarders. Boarders had only one way into the ship during battle—through the turret—and they would have been easy targets for small arms fire on the flat deck. By the time the Confederates could try boarding, the *Monitor* had steamed out of close proximity.

Captain Worden now decided to ram the *Virginia*. Worden sensed that a well-aimed strike at the stern would have disabled the *Virginia*'s propeller and rudder, basically wrecking the ship for further combat. Worden's ship headed full speed toward its target, but just before the two ships collided, the *Monitor*'s steering malfunctioned, causing it to miss the target. The Confederates thought that if the *Monitor* had hit, the battle would have been over.

As the *Monitor* passed, Jones ordered the stern gun to fire at a range of about 20 yards (18 meters). This shot hit the pilothouse, cracking the second iron log from the top and bending back the iron cover several inches. The shot exploded practically in the face of Captain Worden. For the time being at least, Worden was blind. At Worden's instructions, Keller went to get Greene. Worden explained to Greene what had happened and turned over command. Worden's only instruction to Greene was to save the *Minnesota*. Greene then helped Worden to his cabin.

Greene and the other officers decided to continue the fight. Meanwhile, the quartermaster who was steering the *Monitor* had turned the ship away from the *Virginia* when Worden was hit. By the time they got the ship turned back around, the *Monitor* had gone into water far too shallow for the *Virginia* to follow. The crew of the *Virginia* saw the *Monitor*'s apparent departure. The men thought the crew was either retreating or trying to lure the *Virginia* into the shoals for some more leisurely pounding.

Jones decided to go after the *Minnesota*. His pilots warned against this, however. Jones was nearly out of time; the tide was already receding, and if he waited much longer, the water would not be deep enough to get over the sandbar at the entrance to the Elizabeth River. Jones, who would have stayed to fight if he had thought the *Monitor* were still going to fight, decided he had no choice but to return to Norfolk.

Greene thought the *Virginia* was retreating. He also had specific orders to defend the *Minnesota*, which did not allow for pursuing the *Virginia* back to Norfolk. The pilothouse could still be used, but another hit might kill everyone in area. Captain Worden was seriously wounded and needed more medical attention than he could get on board the ship. Greene broke off action and returned to the *Minnesota*. At about 12:30 P.M., on March 9, 1862, one of the most influential battles in naval history had ended.

"March 10," Meaning and Postscript

The U.S.S. *Monitor* gave its name not just to a class of ships, but it became one of the rare vessels in naval history to give its name to a *type*, the "monitors." Several later monitors are shown in this lithograph from a naval history published in 1897.

THE MEANING OF THE BATTLE

Between 6:00 and 7:00 P.M. on Sunday, March 9, 1862, Assistant Secretary of the Navy Gustavus V. Fox, who had witnessed the battle, sent three telegrams. The battle had ended several hours before but Fox presumably wanted to wait until sundown before sending his news, when he was sure the C.S.S. *Virginia* was not coming back. The first telegram went to the commander of the blockading squadron based in Hampton Roads, who, for the last several months, had been busy directing operations off North Carolina. Fox told him that "After a four-hour's fight the *Monitor* had driven the *Merrimack* away from the *Minnesota*. . . ." Fox added that "[the *Monitor*] is yet uninjured,

97

and my impression is that the *Merrimack* is very little hurt." A similar message went out a few minutes later to Secretary of the Navy Welles. In it, Fox added, "The *Monitor* is uninjured and ready at any moment to repel another attack."[39]

A few moments later, Welles was pithier in a telegram he sent John Ericsson in New York. The entire telegram reads: "Your noble boat has performed with perfect success, and Worden and Stimers have handled her with great skill. She is uninjured."[40] The word *your* was more exact than one might expect. Ericsson had not yet received his final payment, contingent on the ship's proving itself, so he partly owned the warship when it went into battle. Ericsson and his partners soon received their last payment.

Two days later, Confederate Secretary of the Navy Stephen Mallory transmitted Jones's official report to President Jefferson Davis. Mallory ended his covering letter by saying:

> To the dashing courage, the patriotism, and eminent ability of Flag-Officer Buchanan and the officers and men of his squadron our country is indebted for this brilliant achievement, which will hold a conspicuous place among the heroic contests of naval history.[41]

Fox and Mallory were both right. This creates a challenge to analyzing the battle. People tend to look at battles the same way they look at sports games—who won? A battle that ends indecisively can seem as frustrating as a game that ends in a tie. Battles can have different types of results, though, and rarely end in a tie in every aspect.

The *Virginia*'s goal on March 9, 1862, was to continue what it had started the day before by destroying the U.S.S. *Minnesota*, invitingly stuck in the mud in the middle of

Hampton Roads. The *Virginia* failed to destroy its target. Despite not being able to get as close as he liked, due to the very tricky shoals in Hampton Roads, Catesby Jones, the *Virginia*'s acting captain, would have destroyed the *Minnesota* had he been able to concentrate on that task. It just would have taken longer from a mile out than from the preferred half mile out. The damage the *Virginia*'s shots did to the *Minnesota* did from a mile and a half away shows what could have happened.

The *Monitor* diverted Confederate attention, and by doing so, carried out Captain Worden's primary orders from Captain Marston—to protect the *Minnesota*. So, for accomplishing its immediate task when the *Virginia* failed to accomplish its immediate task, score one for the *Monitor*.

The *Virginia*, despite the close call of the midfight grounding, did emerge from the battle with no damage to major parts of the ship. The *Monitor*'s pilothouse, the key to navigation, took a shell hit. The pilothouse could still be used—its damage was only one reason Greene broke off the fight. However, another hit in or near the pilothouse stood a high chance of killing or at least incapacitating the occupants. The points for best condition after the battle would have to go to the *Virginia*.

This might have changed had the battle continued longer. The *Virginia* was sitting higher and higher in the water as it burned coal and used ammunition and gunpowder. The ship weighed less and the protective eaves from the casemate were almost above the level of the water. There was an increasing chance that a shell might hit the vulnerable wooden hull by accident, even if the *Monitor* crew did not notice and start aiming for that area.

The continuing existence of each ship would act as a check on the actions of the other. The *Monitor* could prevent the *Virginia* from attacking the blockading fleet. Had the Union fleet just left Hampton Roads, conceding the area to the Southerners, the Confederates might have had time to solve the problems of the *Virginia*'s unarmored hull and how to lighten the ship and get it out of the Roads area. Stanton's fears for Washington's safety might have ended up justified. On the other side, the *Virginia* prevented the Union forces from trying to retake Norfolk from the sea.

Despite being an apparent draw, the strategic standoff favored the North. The war as a whole required the North to take the offensive. Lincoln and his generals had to actively conquer the South. All the South had to do was avoid being conquered by maintaining the status quo of its existence until the North gave up. The North, however, was not giving up in Hampton Roads, and it was not giving up on the blockade. Though still full of holes, and never perfect, the blockade was increasingly effective. If things stayed the way they were, the Confederates would start to feel the pinch. The blockade would also stand as an increasing sign to foreign powers, particular Great Britain, that Washington had the situation under control. The Confederates had to change things. They did not, and so the strategic victory has to be awarded to the *Monitor*.

Greater than the impact of the Battle of Hampton Roads on the course of the Civil War was its impact on the course of naval design. On March 8, the C.S.S. *Virginia* had little difficulty destroying two large "state of the art" wooden warships. Another ironclad was the only thing that stopped the *Virginia* from destroying three more the next day. The *Virginia*'s armor allowed it time to destroy the *Congress* and the *Cumberland*. The Union gunners on those ships were good at their job, not to mention very dedicated. The *Cumberland* crew, at least, kept firing after the ship was clearly sinking. The *Virginia* was hit numerous times, enough to sink a wooden warship, but it was barely scratched. Not having to worry about dodging enemy fire can be a great advantage for a commander. No fancy maneuvering needed, just steam straight toward the target.

The March 9 battle, the first fight between two ironclads, gave strong evidence of the power of the armor. Even an ironclad, barring a lucky shot, could not sink an ironclad. The *Monitor* crew could not see any apparent damage to convince it to concentrate on the same spot where it had started to crack the *Virginia*'s armor. The vulnerability of the *Monitor*'s pilothouse was corrected in later models. The potential problems with the *Virginia*'s unarmored hull could have been corrected. These weaknesses were minor design errors, not problems with the basic concept.

The *Monitor*'s turret was just as important as the idea of armor. A warship in battle normally had to turn sideways to an enemy and fire a broadside to bring its maximum power to bear on the opponent. Broadside meant becoming a broad target for the enemy, though. It also meant the entire ship had to be maneuvered in close combat. The *Virginia* risked disaster when its close combat maneuvers led it aground. The Confederates built other ironclads with the casemate design of the *Virginia*. The Union navy used a similar design for some ironclads, particularly for use on the rivers. However, the Union concentrated on improving the *Monitor*'s design, including developing seagoing vessels. (The *Monitor* itself was clearly not seagoing.) In fact, the *Monitor* was one of the rare ships to give its name to a type of vessel. Further ships in the same and similar designs were not called *Monitor*-class; they were called "monitors."

The best summary of the effects of this battle on the world's navies may have come a few days later in the *London Times*. Commenting on how easily the American ironclads would be able to handle the pride of the Royal

Navy divers cheer as the turret of the U.S.S. *Monitor* is brought up from the ocean floor off the coast of Cape Hatteras, North Carolina, August 5, 2002, nearly 140 years after the warship sank.

navy, the *Times* added that "Whereas we had available for immediate purposes 149 first-class war-ships, we now have two. . . ."[42]

THE FATES OF THE *MONITOR* AND THE *VIRGINIA*

The high point in the careers of the U.S.S. *Monitor* and the C.S.S. *Virginia* came when they fought each other on March 9, 1862. However, each still had life left.

Almost immediately after battle, the *Virginia* went into dry dock for repairs. About the same time and while still recovering from his wound, Buchanan responded to Mallory's ambitious suggestion that the *Virginia* steam up the coast to attack New York City. Buchanan pointed out all the odds against success, starting with the risk from trying to pass the powerful Union guns at Fort Monroe, at the entrance to Hampton Roads, likely assisted by the *Monitor*. Even if the ship could get over the underwater sandbar at the entrance to the Roads, it was probably not sufficiently seaworthy for an ocean voyage. Even if it could get into New York Harbor, requiring the unlikely chance of finding a local pilot willing to help, the Union could easily block its escape.

By April 11, 1862, the *Virginia* was out of dry dock. The ship had a new commander, Flag Officer Josiah Tattnall. Buchanan was not recovered enough to resume active command and Jones was still considered too young, despite his command of the ship in combat on March 9.

Tattnall had a plan to capture the *Monitor*. The Confederates had noticed that during combat, the *Monitor*'s upper deck, on the other side of where the turret guns were facing, would be a blind spot for the crew. They thought the ship could be boarded if the *Virginia* engaged the *Monitor* and distracted the crew. Selected men would board the ship from four supporting armed steamers. Men would throw blankets over the pilothouse—apparently not thinking that this would alert the crew and quickly bring armed Union sailors on deck—and the smokestack. Water poured down the vents would stop the engines. (This is virtually what had happened on the *Monitor*'s trip south to Hampton Roads.) Wedges would be driven between the turret and the deck, preventing the turret from spinning. Bottles of turpentine would be lit and thrown down the vents and the turret. While all this was going on, the four steamers would throw ropes around the turret, to hold the *Monitor* in place.

The *Monitor* officers suspected that the Confederates might try boarding, so the ship had stocked up on small arms. However, if the Union did not get enough men on deck quickly the Confederate plan had a chance of working.

On April 11, most Union transport ships had left

Hampton Roads and anchored near Fort Monroe. However, three were captured by one of the ships supporting the *Virginia*. The *Monitor* did come into Hampton Roads, but its new captain, William Jeffers, was under orders not to pursue the *Virginia* into the southern part of Hampton Roads. Both commanders also wanted to remain within supporting range of their respective shore batteries. Each ship steamed back and forth for several hours, but nothing happened. Finally, Tattnall fired one shot in the direction of the *Monitor*, a sign of contempt, and steamed away. The *Monitor* crew and its captain were disappointed that they did not get another chance to fight the *Virginia*.

In early May, Union Major General George McClellan began to land 100,000 troops as the first phase of his Peninsula Campaign against Richmond. On May 3, the Confederates ordered the evacuation of Norfolk. The *Virginia* made several forays into Hampton Roads, mostly as a distraction. One of the people to see the Confederate ironclad was Abraham Lincoln, down to visit Fort Monroe at the start of McClellan's campaign. On May 10, Union forces landed by sea near Norfolk, at a spot actually selected by Lincoln, and began to advance on that city. The Confederates left, after burning military stores and equipment that could not be removed, at Norfolk and Gosport Navy Yard.

The commander of the Confederate army forces at Norfolk did not keep his promise to inform Flag Officer Tattnall of his departure. Tattnall had just a few hours to act before finding himself boxed in between Union forces in Norfolk and those in Hampton Roads. The pilots told him that they could get his ship at least partway up the James—an underwater sandbar blocked the entrance—if the ship could be lightened. After several hours of hard work by the crew, the pilots changed their mind and said they could not get the ship into the James. Additionally, the ship was now sitting so high in the water that two feet (half a meter) of unprotected wooden hull, its rudder, and propeller were visible above the waterline. If it got into combat, the ship would no longer really be an ironclad. Tattnall, who realized this, had little choice as to what to do next.

He took his ship a few miles north to Craney Island and grounded it. His men would have a long, but direct, walk to join the Confederate army at Suffolk. Since the ship was still in deep water, it took several hours for the *Virginia*'s two boats to get the men ashore. In a slight violation of naval custom, Catesby Jones was the last to leave. He lit a match to the ship's combustibles, and then quickly headed for shore on the last boat. The men were well into their 22-mile (35-kilometer) walk when they heard the extremely loud explosion that marked the end of the C.S.S. *Virginia*.

The men of the C.S.S. *Virginia*, though not their ship, would get one last shot, literally, at the *Monitor*. On May 15, the crew held artillery positions at Drewry's Bluff, south of Richmond, on the James River. They helped repel an attempt to reach Richmond by water led by the *Monitor* and the U.S.S. *Galena*, one of the other two ironclads resulting from Welles's board the year before.

The men of the U.S.S. *Monitor* spent a quiet, boring summer at Hampton Roads. They got a new captain in August, John P. Bankhead. In early October, the ship was towed to the Washington Navy Yard for repairs. It proved to be a great tourist attraction, particularly on the day the ship was open for visitors. Paymaster Keller at one point that day found some women brushing their hair in his cabin, using his brushes.

On December 29, 1862, the U.S.S. *Rhode Island* took the *Monitor* under tow and headed south to Beaufort,

(continued on page 108)

The Recovery of the U.S.S. *Monitor*

Another unusual aspect of the story of the U.S.S. *Monitor*, a story filled with unusual aspects, is that it did not end when the ship sank on the last day of 1862. Efforts were made to locate the *Monitor* over the next 110 years. In 1973, scientists from Duke University aboard the research vessel *Eastward* went out for another attempt. In August of that year, the scientists narrowed the search area down to a 5-mile by 14-mile (8-kilometer by 23-kilometer) section of the Atlantic Ocean, 20 miles (32 kilometers) southeast of Cape Hatteras, North Carolina — one of the most dangerous areas of water in the world. The leader of the expedition explained that tracing the route taken by the U.S.S. *Rhode Island*, which had been towing the *Monitor* when it sank, enabled the crew to plan its search.

The *Eastward* located 22 wrecks during its search of the target area. Each wreck was compared with the expected "footprint" of the *Monitor*, an estimation of what the ship would look like at the bottom of the sea. Twenty-one of these sites were eliminated. The final site was 16 miles (26 kilometers) south-southeast of the Cape Hatteras lighthouse in 220 feet (67 meters) of water. The size and basic shape matched what the scientists expected to find. However, the technology of the time — depending on a grainy image on a video monitor from a black and white video camera suspended at the end of a cable — made it hard to verify the ship's identity. Further complications came from the fact that the ship was upside down. Five months passed before Duke University could announce that it had found the remains of the U.S.S. *Monitor.*

A second expedition, in April 1974, used a more advanced vessel and cameras. This expedition produced better-quality photo images and these photos were used by the U.S. navy's Naval Intelligence Support Center to produce a complete photo mosaic of the work. This was the final proof needed that the U.S.S. *Monitor* had been found.

The question of what to do with the *Monitor* quickly arose. On January 30, 1975, the remains of the *Monitor* and a one-mile-wide area of water was designated as the first United States National Marine Sanctuary, which allowed the government to control access to the ship. Early research at the site was directed at documenting the wreck, studying how it might be preserved, and studying its effect on marine life in the area. On March 9, 1987, the *Monitor* was declared a National Historic Landmark.

In 2001, an expedition recovered part of the hull and the entire steam engine. A more ambitious expedition, on August 5, 2002, used a metal crane nicknamed "the spider" and brought up what was probably the *Monitor*'s most innovative feature, the revolving turret, and its two guns. Once on shore, the turret was transported for preservation and study to the Mariners' Museum in Newport News, Virginia, not far

Destruction of the C.S.S. Virginia, *off Craney Island, early in the morning on May 11, 1862.*

from where the *Monitor* gained its fame. The human remains found in the turret have been sent to the U.S. army's central identification laboratory, in Hawaii, for possible identification. They will be treated the same way as unknown remains from the Korean and Vietnam wars—as tools to possibly identify personnel missing in action.

Commenting on the recovery of the *Monitor* turret, John B. Hightower, president and chief executive officer of the Mariners' Museum, said, "The recovery of one of the great icons of Civil War technology is an awe-inspiring moment for lovers of history. . . . Americans have their first look since the Civil War at this extraordinary invention that held off a nearly successful fearsome challenge to the Federal Navy. . . . Naval warfare was changed forever. . . ."*

A different perspective came from Commander Barbara L. Scholley, commanding officer of the navy's Mobile Diving and Salvage Unit Two and on-scene commander of the expedition: "Working on the *Monitor* has been a surreal experience. For myself and the rest of the Navy men and women on *Monitor* Expedition 2002, this has been much more than just recovering the turret. It has also been a mission to return home shipmates who lost their lives at sea while serving their country."**

---

*   Quoted in Justin Lyons, "Raising the Turret," *Naval History*, December 2002, web site
    www.uni.org/NavalHistory

** Quoted in Ibid.

The sinking of the U.S.S. *Monitor* on the night of December 30–31, 1862. The U.S.S. *Rhode Island* stands in the background as boats rescue as many members of the *Monitor*'s crew as possible. Line engraving from *Harper's Weekly*, 1863.

(continued from page 105)

North Carolina. The *Monitor* would become part of the blockading fleet. A day later, on the night of December 30, it ran into a severe storm off Cape Hatteras, one of the most dangerous places in the world. The storm was as bad as, or worse than, what the *Monitor* had faced off New Jersey on its way south to Hampton Roads. This time, however, the ship was not so lucky. Just after midnight on December 31, 1862, the U.S.S. *Monitor* sank in 200 feet (61 meters) of water. Sixteen men were killed.

The story of this ship, however, does not even end with its sinking. In late 1973, a Duke University expedition found the *Monitor*, upside down on the sea bottom. Several diving expeditions over the next two years brought up artifacts from the wreck and the ship was then given to the government. (Actually, in accordance with international law, the U.S. navy had always owned it.) In August 2002, a government-sponsored expedition brought the *Monitor*'s most innovative feature, its turret, to the surface. At the time that this book was written, and likely for some time after that, the contents of the turret were being examined and studied at the Mariners' Museum in Newport News, Virginia, ironically near the birthplace of its rival, the C.S.S. *Virginia*. Among the contents found in the turret were two human skeletons.

1861

April 17	Virginia Secession Convention votes to secede from the Union.
April 19	Norfolk (Gosport) Navy Yard is abandoned by Union forces. U.S.S. *Merrimack*, burned by Union forces, sinks in the Elizabeth River.
June 23	Confederates propose using the retrieved hulk of the *Merrimack* as the basis for an ironclad vessel.
October 4	John Ericsson signs contract to build a Union ironclad, later called the U.S.S. *Monitor*.

1862

February 17	C.S.S. *Virginia* is commissioned.
February 25	U.S.S. *Monitor* is commissioned.
March 6	*Monitor* leaves New York Harbor on its journey to Hampton Roads, Virginia.
March 8	First day of the naval Battle of Hampton Roads. *Virginia* rams and sinks U.S.S. *Cumberland* and sets fire to U.S.S. *Congress*, which blows up just after midnight on March 9, 1862.
March 9	Second day of the Battle of Hampton Roads. U.S.S. *Monitor* and C.S.S. *Virginia* fight to a draw. This is the first battle between two ironclad vessels.
March 21	Flag Officer Josiah Tattnall becomes second commander of C.S.S. *Virginia*, replacing Flag Officer Franklin Buchanan.
May 10	The city of Norfolk falls to Union forces.
May 11	C.S.S. *Virginia* destroyed.
May 15	U.S.S. *Monitor* is among the Union vessels to shell Drewry's Bluff, near Richmond. This is the last combat for the *Monitor*.
December 31	U.S.S. *Monitor* sinks off Cape Hatteras, North Carolina.

2002

August 6	Turret and guns of *Monitor* are recovered from ocean bottom and brought to shore for study and preservation.

CHAPTER 1: THE FALL OF THE GOSPORT NAVY YARD

1. David Detzer, *Allegiance: Fort Sumter, Charleston, and the Beginning of the Civil War*, New York: Harcourt, Inc., 2001, quoted on p. 269.
2. James M. McPherson, *Battle Cry of Freedom: The Civil War Era*, New York: Oxford University Press, 1988, quoted on p. 294.
3. Quoted at web site *http://www.civilwarhome.com*

CHAPTER 2: THE BIRTH OF THE C.S.S. *VIRGINIA*

4. William C. Davis, *Duel Between the First Ironclads*, Baton Rouge: Louisiana State University Press, 1981, quoted on p. 8.
5. United States Department of the Navy, *Official Records of the Union and Confederate Navies in the War of the Rebellion*, Washington, D.C.: Government Printing Office, 1894–1922.
6. Davis, quoted on p. 9.
7. John M. Brooke, "The Plan and Construction of the 'Merrimac' I," in Robert U. Johnson and C. C. Buel, eds., *Battles and Leaders of the Civil War*, New York: Century, 1888, vol. 1, p. 715.
8. Davis, p. 10.
9. John L. Porter, "The Plan and Construction of the 'Merrimac' II," in Robert U. Johnson and C. C. Buel, eds., *Battles and Leaders of the Civil War*, New York: Century, 1888, vol. 1, p. 717.
10. Davis, quoted on p. 12.
11. H. Ashton Ramsey, "Most Famous of Sea Duels: The Merrimac and Monitor," *Harper's Weekly*, February 10, 1912, p. 11.
12. *Official Records of the Union and Confederate Navies*, vol. 2, p. 175.

CHAPTER 3: THE BIRTH OF THE U.S.S. *MONITOR*

13. William C. Davis, *Duel Between the First Ironclads*, Baton Rouge: Louisiana State University Press, 1981, p. 15.
14. "Negotiations for the Building of the 'Monitor'," in Robert U. Johnson and C. C. Buel, eds., *Battles and Leaders of the Civil War*, vol. 1, Century, 1888, p. 748.
15. A. A. Hoehling, *Thunder at Hampton Roads*, Englewood Cliffs, NJ: Prentice-Hall, Inc., 1976, quoted on p. 46.
16. "Negotiations for the Building of the 'Monitor'," vol. 1, p. 749.
17. Davis, quoted on p. 43.

CHAPTER 4: GETTING TO WAR

18. James Tertius de Kay, *Monitor: The Story of the Legendary Civil War Ironclad and the Man Whose Invention Changed the Course of History*, New York: Walker and Company, 1997, p. 112.
19. Daly, Robert W., *Aboard the USS Monitor: 1862, The Letters of Acting Paymaster William Frederick Keeler, U.S. Navy, To His Wife, Anna*, Annapolis, MD: United States Naval Institute, 1964.

20. Allan C. Stimers, "An Engineer Aboard the Monitor," *Civil War Times Illustrated*, vol. IX, April 1970, pp. 29–30.
21. Samuel Dana Greene, "In the Monitor Turret," in Robert U. Johnson and C. C. Buel, eds., *Battles and Leaders of the Civil War*, vol. 1, Century, 1888, p. 720.
22. Stimers, pp. 29–30.
23. Ibid.
24. Daly, pp. 30–31.

CHAPTER 5: MARCH 8

25. William C. Davis, *Duel Between the First Ironclads*, Baton Rouge: Louisiana State University Press, 1981, quoted on p. 75.
26. H. Ashton Ramsey, "Most Famous of Sea Duels: The Merrimac and Monitor," *Harper's Weekly*, February 10, 1912, p. 11.
27. A. A. Hoehling, *Thunder at Hampton Roads*, Englewood Cliffs, NJ: Prentice-Hall, Inc., 1976, quoted on p. 105.
28. *New York Times*, March 14, 1862.
29. R. E. Colston, "Watching the 'Merrimac'," in Robert U. Johnson and C. C. Buel, eds., *Battles and Leaders of the Civil War*, vol. 1, Century, 1888, p. 713.
30. Ibid.
31. *New York Times*, March 14, 1862.
32. Hoehling, quoted on p. 112.

CHAPTER 6: MARCH 9

33. Gideon Welles, *Diary of Gideon Welles*, with an introduction by John T. Morse, Jr., Boston and New York: Houghton Mifflin Company, The Riverside Press, Cambridge, 1911, pp. 62, 64.
34. John Taylor Wood, "The First Fight of the Iron-Clads," in Robert U. Johnson and C. C. Buel, eds., *Battles and Leaders of the Civil War*, vol. 1, Century, 1888, p. 701.
35. E. Shippen, "Two Battle Pictures," *The United Service*, vol. IV, January 1881, pp. 62–63.
36. William Norris, "The Story of the Confederate States Ship Virginia . . .", *Southern Historical Society Papers*, vol. XLII, October 1917, p.211.
37. William C. Davis, *Duel Between the First Ironclads*, Baton Rouge: Louisiana State University Press, 1981, quoted on pp. 127–128.

CHAPTER 7: "MARCH 10," MEANING AND POSTSCRIPT

38. Daly, Robert W., *Aboard the USS Monitor: 1862, The Letters of Acting Paymaster William Frederick Keeler, U.S. Navy, To His Wife, Anna*, Annapolis, MD: United States Naval Institute, 1964.
39. Ibid., p. 7.
40. Ibid., pp. 41–42.
41. Mark St. John Erickson, "Sunken Ambition," *Daily Press*, Hampton Roads, VA, January 3, 1998.

Brooke, John M., "The Plan and Construction of the 'Merrimac' I," *Battles and Leaders of the Civil War,* ed. Robert U. Johnson and C. C. Buel, Volume I, New York: Century, 1888.

Bushnell, Cornelius S., et al., "Negotiations for the Building of the 'Monitor,'" *Battles and Leaders of the Civil War,* ed. Robert U. Johnson and C. C. Buel, Volume I, New York: Century, 1888.

Campbell, R. Thomas, and Alan B. Flanders, *Confederate Phoenix: The CSS Virginia,* Shippensburg, PA: Burd Street Press, 2001.

CNN.com/US., "Monitor Turret Raised from Ocean," *www.cnn.com,* August 6, 2002

Colston, R. E., "Watching the 'Merrimac,'" *Battles and Leaders of the Civil War,* ed. Robert U. Johnson and C. C. Buel, Volume I, New York: Century, 1888, pp. 712–714.

Davis, William C., *Duel Between the First Ironclads,* Baton Rouge: Louisiana State University Press, 1981.

Detzer, David, *Allegiance: Fort Sumter, Charleston, and the Beginning of the Civil War,* New York: Harcourt, Inc., 2001.

Durkin, Joseph T., S.J. *Confederate Navy Chief: Stephen R. Mallory,* Columbia, SC: University of South Carolina Press, 1954.

Erickson, Mark St. John, "Sunken Ambition," *Daily Press,* Hampton Roads, VA: January 3, 1988.

Fiscor, Steve, (Editorial Director, *Mining,* Primedia Business Mining and Construction Group), e-mails to author of October 28, 2002, and October 30, 2002.

Fowler, William M. Jr., *Under Two Flags: The American Navy in the Civil War,* New York and London: W. W. Norton & Co., 1990.

Gentile, Gary, *Ironclad Legacy: Battles of the USS Monitor,* Philadelphia, PA: Gary Gentile Productions, 1993.

Greene, Samuel Dana, "In the Monitor Turret," *Battles and Leaders of the Civil War,* ed. Robert U. Johnson and C. C. Buel, Volume I, New York: Century, 1888.

Hoehling, A. A., *Thunder at Hampton Roads,* Englewood Cliffs, NJ: Prentice-Hall, Inc., 1976.

Konstam, Angus, *Hampton Roads, 1862,* London: Osprey Publishing Company, 1992.

Lienhard, John H., *Engines of Our Ingenuity,* Episode 1344, "The Monitor's Flush Toilet," web site www.uh.edu/engines.

Lyons, Justin, "Raising the Turret," *Naval History,* December 2002, web site *www.usni.org/Naval History.*

McKay, James Tertius, *Monitor: The Story of the Legendary Civil War Ironclad and the Man Whose Invention Changed the Course of History,* New York: Walker and Company, 1997.

McPherson, James M., *Battle Cry of Freedom: The Civil War Era,* New York and Oxford: Oxford University Press, 1988.

Monitor National Marine Sanctuary, "Monitor Research Plan," *www.moniotr.nos.noaa.gov*, accessed July 2002.

Musicant, Ivan, *Divided Waters: The Naval History of the Civil War*, New York: Harper-Collins Publishers, 1995.

New York Times, March 14, 1862.

NOAA Ocean Explorer, Monitor Expedition 2002, Background, *www.oceanexplorer.noaa.gov/explorations*, July 2002.

NOAA Ocean Explorer, Monitor Expedition 2002, logs, *www.oceanexplorer.noaa.gov/explorations*, logs dated August 6, 2002; July 26, 2002; July 25, 2002; July 24, 2002; July 22, 2002; July 20, 2002; July 13, 2002; July 12, 2002; July 10, 2002; July 5, 2002; June 30, 2002; June 26, 2002; June 25, 2002.

Norris, William, "The Story of the Confederate States Ship *Virginia* . . ." *Southern Historical Society Papers*, XLII, October 1917.

Porter, John L., "The Plan and Construction of the 'Merrimac' II," *Battles and Leaders of the Civil War,* ed. Robert U. Johnson and C. C. Buel, Volume I, New York: Century, 1888.

Ramsay, H. Ashton, "Most Famous of Sea Duels: The Merrimac and the Monitor," *Harper's Weekly*, Volume 61, February 10, 1912.

Shippen, Edward, "Two Battle Pictures," *The United Service,* IV, January 1881.

Shotgun's Home of the American Civil War, *The American Civil War*, "Naval War: Birth of the Ironclads," www.civilwarhome.com/navalwar.htm.

Sifakis, Steward, *Who Was Who in the Civil War*, New York: Facts on File Publications, 1988.

Stimers, Alban C., "An Engineer Aboard the Monitor," *Civil War Times Illustrated*, Volume IX, April 1970.

United States Navy Department, *Official Records of the Union and Confederate Navies in the War of the Rebellion*, 31 Volumes, Washington, D.C.: Government Printing Office, 1884–1927.

USS *Monitor* Center, The Mariners' Museum, "USS Monitor Center Update," periodic mass e-mails, August–November 2002.

Welles, Gideon, *Dairy of Gideon Welles*, with an introduction by John T. Meese, Jr., Boston and New York: Houghton Mifflin Company, the Riverside Press, Cambridge, 1911.

Williamson, Cathy, (Public Services Librarian, the library at the Mariners' Museum) e-mail to author, August 22, 2002.

Worden, J. L., Lieut. U.S.N., Lieut. U.S.N. Greene, and H. Ashton Ramsay, C.S.N., *The Monitor and the Merrimac: Both Sides of the Story*, New York and London: Harper & Brothers, Publishers, 1912.

Bathe, Greville, *Ship of Destiny: A Record of the Steam Frigate Merrimac, 1855–1862,* Philadelphia: Allen, Lane and Scott, 1953.

Baxter, James M., *The Introduction of the Ironclad Warship*, Cambridge: Harvard University Press, 1933.

Coombe, Jack D., *Gunsmoke Over the Atlantic,* New York: Bantam Books, 2002.

Delgado, James P., *A Symbol of American Ingenuity: Assessing the Significance of U.S.S. Monitor*, Washington, D.C.: National Park Service, 1988.

Jones, Virgil C., *The Civil War at Sea,* 3 Volumes, New York: Holt, Rinehart, and Winston, 1960–1962.

Klein, Maury, *Days of Defiance: Sumter, Secession, and the Coming of the Civil War*, New York: Alfred A. Knopf, 1997.

Lauer, Conrad Newton, *John Ericsson, Engineer,* Glenloch, PA: A Newcomen Publication, 1939.

Sears, Stephen W., *To the Gates of Richmond: The Peninsula Campaign*, New York: Ticknor & Fields, 1992.

Stern, Philip Van Doren, *The Confederate Navy: A Pictorial History*, New York: Bonanza Books, 1962.

Weigley, Russell F., *A Great Civil War: A Military and Political History*, Bloomington and Indianapolis: Indiana University Press, 2002.

CONTRIBUTORS

Bruce L. Brager has worked for many years as a staff or freelance writer/editor, specializing in history, political science, foreign policy, energy, and defense/military topics. This is his fourth book, his third book for young adults. His previous book is *The Siege of Petersburg* (published January 2003, Chelsea House), the story of the deciding campaign of the American Civil War. Brager has published more than 50 articles for the general and specialized history markets, the bulk of them on the American Civil War. He was raised in the Washington, D.C., area and New York City. Brager graduated from George Washington University, and currently lives in Arlington, Virginia.

Caspar W. Weinberger was the fifteenth secretary of defense, serving under President Ronald Reagan from 1981 to 1987. Born in California in 1917, he fought in the Pacific during World War II, then went on to pursue a law career. He became an active member of the California Republican Party and was named the party's chairman in 1962. Over the next decade, Weinberger held several federal government offices, including chairman of the Federal Trade Commission and secretary of health, education, and welfare. Ronald Reagan appointed him to be secretary of defense in 1981. He became one of the most respected secretaries of defense in history and served longer than any previous secretary except for Robert McNamara (who served 1961–1968). Today, Weinberger is chairman of the influential *Forbes* magazine.

DATE DUE